Jesus on Trial

JESUS on TRIAL

A Study of the Gospels
2nd Edition

Gerard S. Sloyan

Fortress Press   Minneapolis

Library of Congress Cataloging-in-Publication Data

Sloyan, Gerard Stephen, 1919-
   Jesus on trial : a study of the gospels / Gerard S. Sloyan. — 2nd ed.
     p. cm.
   Includes bibliographical references (p.   ) and index.
   ISBN 978-0-8006-3829-0 (alk. paper)
     1. Jesus Christ—Trial. 2. Jesus Christ—Passion—Role of Jews.
   3. Passion narratives (Gospels)—Criticism, interpretation, etc.
   I. Title.
   BT440.S56 2006
   232.96'2—dc22
                                          2005033863

CONTENTS

ABBREVIATIONS

Ant.	*Antiquities of the Jewish People,* by Josephus (Greek text and Eng. trans. in Loeb Classical Library, Josephus, vols. 4–9, 1930–65)
CBQ	*Catholic Biblical Quarterly*
HTR	*Harvard Theological Review*
JBL	*Journal of Biblical Literature*
JTS NS	*Journal of Theological Studies* (New Series)
JW	*Jewish War (Bellum Judaicum),* by Josephus (Greek text and Eng. trans. in Loeb Classical Library, Josephus, vols. 2–3, 1927–28)
LXX	Septuagint
NAB	New American Bible
NovT	*Novum Testamentum*
NRSV	New Revised Standard Version
n.s.	new series
NT Abstracts	*New Testament Abstracts* (cited by volume number)
NTS	*New Testament Studies*
par., pars.	parallel, parallels (in the Gospels)
PG	Patrologia graeca, ed. J.-P. Migne. 162 vols. Paris, 1857–1886.
Q	*Quelle* or sayings source
RB	*Revue Biblique*
REB	Revised English Bible
Sanh.	*Sanhedrin*
SBT	*Studies in Biblical Theology*
SNTSMS	Society for New Testament Studies Monograph Series (New York: Cambridge University Press)
SQ	*Semeia-Quelle*
TDNT	*Theological Dictionary of the New Testament,* eds. G. Kittel and G. Friedrich (Grand Rapids: Eerdmans, 1964-1976)
ZNW	*Zeitschrift für die Neutestamentlichen Wissenschaft*

Chapter 1

SCHOLARSHIP REGARDING JESUS' SENTENCE to DEATH

W hy should anyone write about the inquest and trial of Jesus?[1] There are several reasons that are self-evident and some others that are not. Of the two sets of reasons, the latter are probably the more influential in producing literary activity about the trial.

As to reasons that are self-evident, the first is that a much-loved and highly respected figure was put to death as a criminal after a judicial process of some sort. The victim is one who has come to be hailed as the founder of a religious tradition. Certain early adherents to this tradition left written accounts of the events that led to his execution. That these accounts should be examined with scholarly care seems to be the most natural thing in the world, if only because all of the extant literature of the Christians, canonical and uncanonical alike, has been subjected to a critical scrutiny over the last two centuries.

Besides this general concern for the final days of a Great One and the specific concern of those who believe in him to submit their Scriptures to literary criticism because of the scientific spirit of the age—reasons which I have termed self-evident—there are other, more compelling factors at work that have resulted in a literature on the trial of Jesus. Christians are committed by doctrinal (sometimes the word "dogmatic" is used) principle to the historical dependability in some sense or other of their canonical Scriptures. This means that any strong indication from within these writings of tendentious activity or the nonhistorical character of details is likely to elicit a defensive response from Christians.

SOME HISTORICAL and THEOLOGICAL PRESUPPOSITIONS

In the case of the trial, the response derives from a faith commitment to the dependability of this literature that originates outside the literature itself. It would go something like this: the church (through which Christians believe) has taught that the Gospels are true; hence the seemingly historical details contained in them are true, and in particular the details about Jesus' redeeming death.

The Gospels attribute ultimate responsibility[2] for the death sentence of Jesus to the Romans through their civil servant (called a "prefect" in Jesus' day but later a "procurator"; also in the Greek of the Gospels *hēgemōn*, "governor"), Pontius Pilate. They also cite the complicity of various leadership elements in the Jewish community, chiefly the Temple priests but also in a mention or two the Pharisees. The apologetic stance with regard to such an account will include the necessity of maintaining that there was, indeed, such complicity even if it did not take the exact form indicated by the Gospels—documents widely admitted by Christian scholars to have been written from a faith standpoint.

A contemporary Christian apologetic motive for writing about the trial that may be totally unconscious in those it motivates is the need to retain some Jewish guilt for Jesus' death and not only Gentile guilt. The overt reason alleged is that the Gospels say that various influential elements within the Jewish people impelled the Romans to action and the Gospels cannot be wrong in a matter of such importance.[3] The covert reason is that the guilt of Jewish Temple and Sanhedrin leadership is thought to be a matter of such importance. In other words, the claim that there was some Jewish responsibility for Jesus' death is conceived to be part of the substance of Christian faith, when in fact, apart from the membership of Jews in a sinful humanity, it is not.[4] All that Christian faith requires is that Jesus died for the sins of the entire human race. At whose hands is of no consequence. The deed was done by sinful humanity taken globally.

If Christians are thus unconsciously motivated with respect to writing about the trial, they may be consciously motivated by a reverse apologetic, namely, the desire to provide an *amende honorable.* This they could accomplish by arguing that since only a Roman sentence of "guilty" could have resulted in Jesus' execution, any other influences reported in the Gospels are suspect as tendentious and unhistorical.

The various Jewish inclinations in this whole matter should be as clear as the Christian. Since Jews have endured so much suffering at Christian hands over the matter of Jesus, and since the Gospel accounts of a Jewish judicial process—apparently more a hearing than a trial—give evidence of being garbled, the Jewish writer may be expected to point out that there is more anti-Jewish polemic in the trial narratives than there is familiarity with Jewish legal procedure as it can be reconstructed from Talmudic sources.

An occasional Jewish response to the question, however, falls outside of the expected categories. Thus, Samuel Sandmel confesses himself unable to have any view on the historicity of the trial because the documents available, the Gospels, do not possess enough historical character to help him construct a historical argument one way or the other. He writes:

> The point is *not at all* that I regard the Gospel material on the trial of Jesus as devoid of all historical basis, and as only a tissue of legend and of *Tendenz.* The case, rather, is

that I simply do not know how, as a historian, I can separate whatever may be the kernel of historical reality from the other material which I am convinced is not historically accurate. In short, I give up on the problem.[5]

Rabbi Sandmel, who was Professor of Bible and Hellenistic Literature at Hebrew Union College, Cincinnati, concludes the account of his historical agnosticism with the observation that the problem surrounding the trial is, after all, a Christian problem, not a Jewish one. As a Jew, he need not have a view, and if he did, it probably would not affect him, his wife, and his children. They are secure in the knowledge that they had no part in the high priest's interrogation. He speculates that if, by some marvel, the truth about it were at last to become known the impact would be minimal, since "historical scholarship is almost powerless against the persistence of motifs in a religious tradition, whether it be Christianity or Judaism."[6] There is little harm in books on the subject, Sandmel thinks, but also little utility. Sentiments of one religious group against another are, by and large, ineradicable.

A Jewish position on the trial that is unusual is that of Associate Justice Haim Cohn of the Supreme Court of Israel who in 1968 published a book in Hebrew on the question.[7] Numerous jurists, Christian, Jewish, and unaffiliated, have published studies on this topic, so Justice Cohn is not distinguished by his interest. It is rather his opinion which sets him apart. In brief, it is that the Sanhedrin—a largely Sadducean group that did not enjoy the confidence of the people—tried to prevent the execution of Jesus and bring about his acquittal, or at least a suspended sentence, by persuading him not to plead guilty; that is, not to persist in claims that could be taken as seditious by the Romans.

> I submit that there can have been only one thing in which the Jewish leadership of the day was vitally interested: it was *to prevent* the execution by the Romans of a Jew (and a Pharisee) who happened to enjoy the affection and love of the people. Their motives were realistic and political. . . .

While the Sanhedrin had thus to be watchful not to alien-
ate such good will of the Roman authorities as it could still
enjoy, the first and foremost condition for its survival and
effectiveness was to retain the confidence and loyalty of
the people. . . . In the light of this purpose [viz., to be able
to produce reliable witnesses to prove Jesus' innocence
and to assume responsibility toward the Roman procurator for the future good behavior of Jesus], the events of
that night [the reported meeting of the Sanhedrin] are
readily explained and understood.[8]

The Israeli author is aware that his case rests heavily on the
argument from silence, namely, the silence (or paucity) of Jewish
sources. Nonetheless, he employs details in the Gospels such as the
examination of witnesses and the high priest's tearing of his garments to make his case. The testimony the Council heard against
Jesus was, as the Gospels say using other words, "false and inad-
missible. Hence it so found and declared."[9] But the nonavailability
of witnesses was not enough to secure a man's freedom in Roman
law, as it was in Jewish law, where reliable evidence from at least
two eyewitnesses was required. In Roman practice the accused's
own utterance was sufficient to condemn him.

The first step, according to Cohn, was therefore to discredit any
persons who would testify against Jesus falsely. The second was to
save him from himself by dissuading him from pleading guilty or
engaging in any self-incriminating speech. But when Jesus admitted to being "the Christ, the Son of the Blessed" (Mark 14:61) and
spoke of himself in the words of Daniel 7 as "the Son of Man sitting
on the right hand of the Power" (Mark 14:62), the high priest rent
his clothes, not at blasphemy, but in grief: "it was because of his
failure to make Jesus see his point and cooperate, and because of
the impending doom."[10]

Justice Cohn is familiar with the quite different use the Evangelists later made of the data he employs. He knows that by the
time they came to write they saw the Sanhedrin as the enemy; that,
as part of what he takes to be an increasingly Gentile church, they

no longer recognize the biblical importance of getting the testimony of two witnesses who will agree (Matthew is an exception, although in other contexts; see 18:16, 20), nor the terms of blasphemy, nor the tearing of garments in sorrow. He also requires that three supposed references to Jesus' trial in the Talmud be recognized as not germane to it.[11] Above all, his theory demands the general dependability of both the historical tradition of a Jewish hearing and of some of its specific details. This dependability, coupled with speculation on what would best ensure the survival of the power class, are the ingredients of his ingenious construct.

Some contemporary interest in the trial falls outside any apologetic purview, or at least any conscious one. It stems from the notion, so congenial to the popular imagination of a few decades ago (think of Che Guevara indistinguishable from Jesus in poster art), that Jesus was a revolutionary whose crime was overt activity against the Roman state. If his was a religious-nationalist stance, several birds could then be killed with one stone. First, Jesus could be the popular hero that some among contemporary youth crave, an antiestablishment figure whose personal convictions required him to pay the ultimate price. Also, his concerns would have been political or secular as much as religious, chiefly the freedom of his people. Finally, the devils of the piece would have been the callous imperial authorities, not an identifiable group of religionists belonging to a tradition and a people still alive today.

The writings of the late Professor S. G. F. Brandon of the University of Manchester, a former British military chaplain, did much for a season to make this theory attractive, but not so attractive that it won wide acceptance in the world of scholarship. Many are indebted to Brandon for his stress on the political aspects of what the Evangelists identify as simply a religious question. It is widely accepted that the Gospels are primarily religious interpretations of Jesus' life and death but not so widely granted that a political dynamic was at work. Brandon proposes the thesis that a late-first-century defense of the Christian community was uppermost in the Evangelists' minds. It would not favor their cause to have the empire know Jesus for the insurgent that he was. Moreover, the priesthood and the Sanhedrin or Great Council had become a far less potent force than the Romans in the lives of the Christians after the destruction of the Temple.

The Gospel accounts, it has correctly been held, constituted, above all, an "existentialist" literature, meaning that they were framed in a way that would meet the life situation of the intended earliest readers. The Gospels were not "historical" in the modern sense. While ostensibly the story of Jesus of Nazareth of *then,* they were in reality an interpretation of the significance of Jesus as Lord and Christ of the Evangelists' *now.* As a contemporary figure in the years 70 through 100 CE, Jesus would have had no religious meaning outside Judaea in terms of an armed revolt. That of 66–70 had been crushed, that of Bar Kokhba of 132–35 had not yet been mounted. Thus, briefly, Professor Brandon argues: the historical fact of Jesus' political concern was suppressed; in its place stress was laid on the savior figure that the writings of Paul can be assumed to have brought into existence.[12]

A SCHOLARLY "BENT" in ALL WRITING on the TRIAL?

The foregoing analysis of various reasons why people write about the trial of Jesus stands as an invitation to the writer to face his own motivations. It might seem to be enough to say that New Testament scholarship is interested in this question, therefore the present writer is. Yet, as Professor Sandmel states, Christian scholars inevitably approach the trial from a point of view: "The trial of Jesus is not really a historical problem, but a problem in apologetics."[13] Anyone, of any religious persuasion or none, who supposes he comes at it with a critical-historical perspective only is self-deceived. What Sandmel calls a "bent" is at work in all scholarship. In this question, he says, it can take the form of salvaging historical authenticity out of the debris which the very scholars' "analytical scholarship has made of the traditional materials."[14] The honest critic comes to be convinced, in other words, that the historical character of the night trial before the Sanhedrin (like the creation narrative in Genesis or the revelation at Sinai) is almost nil. Nonetheless, according to

Sandmel, the believer in Jesus continues to exegete each passage soberly as if the narratives had acquired a historical worth in the aggregate that the individual phrases do not possess.

This much should be evident to any reader of the voluminous critical scholarship on the inquest and trial: even the best of it depends heavily on speculation and reconstruction. Since the events reported obviously did not take place in the form reported—as the simple absence of Christian witnesses at the legal proceedings (cf. Mark 14:54; 15:1 and pars.; John 18:15, 33) and the heavy dependence of the Passion narratives on Psalms 22 and 69 are sufficient to establish—the historical question is, What did in fact take place? Whoever provides an answer is bound to do so on the basis of certain assumptions about the historical character of the Gospels and the theological thrust underlying them. Thus, on historical grounds John's dating of the crucifixion of Jesus on the preparation day for the Passover (John 18:28; 19:31), the 14th Nisan, is more acceptable to some writers than the Synoptic authors' choice of the feast day itself, the 15th. They likewise welcome John's use (at 18:12) of the terms "cohort" and "tribune officer" because they are correct terms for the Roman army; they credit John with a knowledge (19:12) of the technical term "friend of Caesar" for the PHILOKAISAR of inscriptions on the coins of Herod Agrippa I, 37–44 CE; and in general they applaud his familiarity with Jerusalem landmarks like the praetorium (18:28), wherever it was, the Stone Pavement (19:13), and the place of the Skull (19:17). The question to be asked of such writers is whether they have made an act of trust in the fourth Evangelist as a reliable transmitter of tradition generally, or only at those points where his data confirm their presuppositions. Other writers—but far fewer at the present time in scholarship—find John historically worthless, again in terms of their presuppositions.

In general, the question to be posed to all who write on the trial narratives is what their principles are for accepting or rejecting certain passages as historically trustworthy. If all of Josephus, all Talmudic writing, and all Roman law from Justinian's time onward are to be taken as normative, and the Gospels are to be

taken as falling under the judgment of these later-written documents (Josephus' *Jewish War*, dated 77–78 CE, constitutes a partial
exception), some reason needs to be alleged that is more compelling than the simple dismissal of the Gospels as a "faith literature."
Conversely, one may ask whether a New Testament affirmation is
to be assumed historically true until the contrary is proved.

In sum, what norms should be applied in passing judgment
on New Testament statements? One puts these questions because
much reading in the literature begets the uneasy feeling that—
aside from a few total skeptics or an equal number of total accept-
ers of the details contained in the Gospels—many writers have not
thought out their own criteria. They attack the problem with the
general intention of getting at the historical truth of things, then
allow or disallow particular statements in the Gospels in terms not
only of the historical difficulties they know have been raised but
also of what they presuppose could or could not have happened.

There are those, for example, who think that Roman-Sadducean
collaboration was likely, and others who are convinced that any
account whatever of Jewish cooperation with the empire must have
been fabricated. Some will credit all Gospel references to imperial
legal process and discredit any to Jewish, and vice versa. Numerous writers are aware of the heavy influence of the Jewish Scriptures in the Septuagint version on New Testament composition,
while others are not so sensitive. The latter are continually led into
accepting as historical passages that are unquestionably typological. A well-known example is the response to Pilate in Matthew,
at 27:25, "The whole people said in reply, 'Let his blood be on us
and on our children'"; this may derive from Jeremiah 26:15, "But
mark well: if you put me to death, it is innocent blood you bring
on yourselves, on this city and its citizens," perhaps coupled with
51:35 in the same book:

> My torn flesh be upon Babylon,
> says the city of Zion;
> My blood upon the people of Chaldea,
> says Jerusalem.

Finally, there is the almost universal tendency to frame a perfect theory that will adequately account for the details reported in all four Gospels. For many writers, it is not enough to say—what seems to be the fact—that the various Evangelists have a certain number of historical data which they put forward in a theological and perhaps apologetic way. Rather, once this has been said, every detail and discrepancy must be accounted for in terms of some master scheme that is the work of the one writing on the trial. Often the most crucial scholarly declarations go undocumented and are accompanied by the scholar's weakest refuge, the adverb "undoubtedly" or "beyond question." Gospel statements, in a word, are accepted when they fit the modern author's scheme and rejected when they do not.

To say this is not to charge bias so much as to indicate that when anyone wishes to take a stand on what happened at any point in the interrogation and trial sequence, as distinct from what the Evangelists with their conflicting details maintain took place, he or she will do so on the basis of a theory. Individual passages will then be argued in light of this theory. The best theories will result from a sum of probabilities, the worst from what the theorizer wishes had taken place. Thus, there are those who tend to accept unquestioningly the notion of violence done to the person of Jesus, the haste in which he was dealt with, and the exception to ordinary legal processes (the impression given by the Gospels) which his case constituted. There are likewise those who reject as unhistorical any procedures such as the ones reported.

It should be said at the outset that there is no compelling reason for or against such unusual procedures, neither the prima facie evidence of the Gospels nor the later, Talmudic legal specifications. We are in the dark because it is the very nature of an exception, if such the hearing of Jesus before Jewish authority was, to be exceptional. We may either theorize or, taking Professor Sandmel's counsel, refuse to theorize. We should, in any case, be conscious of what we are doing.

One last problem in writings about the trial arises from critical scholarship itself, whether engaged in from a faith standpoint or not. The presupposition of all Gospel exegesis of the last one hundred years has been that each Evangelist had sources, written and oral, and that his literary product was a mosaic of these sources. Tracking them was the primary business of Gospel scholarship, since history was the primary category in biblical research. More recently it has come to be realized that each Evangelist was a storyteller or, better still, a homilist, with respect to his local church. This could mean that an exploration of the art of narrative in each of the four cases is more important than all the labor that has gone into source criticism. The latter endeavor has traditionally been called literary criticism. This would bring a puzzled frown to the face of any genuine littérateur. Now it is seen that examining the Gospels from the standpoint of the Hellenist–Jewish literary writing that they are is the better way to go.

The KIND of WRITING THAT the GOSPELS ARE

Having laid down such strictures against others, the present writer may have made it methodologically impossible for himself to continue. Nonetheless, he will try to list the motives, principles, and presuppositions that he knows or thinks are at work as he sets about his task:

1. The *modern* problem of the trial of Jesus is primarily one of tension between two groups, Christians and Jews. It is such because the existence of these tensions (even though the Christians of the mid-to-late first century CE were in good part ethnic Jews and Gentile God-fearers of the Palestinian heartland and the Diaspora) underlay the composition of the only narratives we have. These narratives, in turn, with their underlying tensions, have contributed to keeping the tensions alive ever since.

2. The problem of the trial of Jesus is only secondarily historical. Something did take place, however discoverable it may or may not be. Accounts of it exist which purport to be historical and which themselves have a history. But the history of the narratives is relatively more available—through form, redaction, and literary criticism understood as narratology—than the history of the

events themselves. It is this *history of the tradition* we shall attempt to explore, to see if it sheds any light on the history of the events.

3. Given the above, something of the actual history of the trial of Jesus is theoretically discoverable. Therefore it should be attempted. It is not to be supposed, however, that inquiring into the historical truth of the matter and producing a finding will automatically result in the reduction of tensions between Christians and Jews. It will contribute to such reduction if it is done in a spirit of truth and love no matter what the findings. If not, it will not so contribute, again no matter what the findings. The relation between Christians and Jews in the present lies outside the realities of past history taken as mere events. From the beginning those relations have not been good because they have been rooted in something other than history as mere event. The disclosures of history cannot be expected to improve them.

What can help is the disclosure of patterns of tension in the past that gave us the accounts we now have. This can encourage Christians to use their Scriptures with more discretion than they have shown up until now: in their selection of pulpit readings, meaning the inclusion of some and the omissions of others; in accommodating the Gospels to other use in a variety of liturgies; in theology, in preaching, and in catechizing.

The literal interpretation of symbolic material—in other words taking metaphor for fact—has probably caused more harm than any other practice in religious life. This seems to be the case in the trial narratives. Facing squarely the fact that these are primarily religious and in some incipient sense theological and not historical documents (i.e., historical in any modern sense—it remains to be seen whether in any sense at all), Christians should then set about using them correctly. That correct use includes a modern mastery of the views the New Testament writers had of ancient symbolism, which in general consisted in a rough correspondence between figures or types out of an older time and subsequent fulfillment as types in the life, death, and resurrection of Jesus.

4. The Evangelists had available to them traditions of judicial or quasi-judicial procedures that had some historical dependability,

not that were totally devoid of it. This we conclude on the basis of what is known from other sources. The trial narratives retain the name of the Roman prefect Pilate, the high priest Caiaphas, his father-in-law Annas (Ḥanan), the requirement under Jewish law that witnesses should agree, the phenomenon of "speaking against the Temple" and sanctions concerning such conduct,[15] the capital punishment of armed insurgents, traitors to the state, and highway robbers, and Pilate's habit of executing swift and severe sentence. All of these matters are testified to elsewhere in writings where the authors are not making any particular case about the last days of Jesus of Nazareth.

5. There may safely be presumed some elements of active hostility to Jesus on the part of certain of his fellow Jews. It would be wrong to suppose otherwise if his public teaching was even remotely like that which the Gospels describe. The activities reported of Jesus—his words and gestures against excesses in Temple worship, chiefly the venality of its administrators, and his predictions of its dissolution in the end time (cf. Matt. 21:12-13; Mark 11:15-19; Luke 19:45-46; John 2:13-22)—could well have secured the opposition of the Temple priesthood. He likewise would have earned the displeasure of some Pharisee teachers if he opposed their legal demands as reported (e.g., Mark 2:6—3:6 passim; Matt. 23:13-36)—the same kinds of excesses as those reprobated in later rabbinic sources.[16]

The Evangelists taken as a whole seem to be unsure of who made up the Sanhedrin, what its judicial competence was, and where the priesthood stood in relation to it. Still, they consistently identify a bloc of Jesus' enemies as the "chief priests," meaning the Temple custodians. It should not surprise us if he had incurred their enmity by his preaching and actions, a hostility which the trial narratives indicate. Importantly, the Pharisees do not appear in any Synoptic accounts of the trial.[17] Mark situates elders and scribes along with chief priests in the high priests' court (14:53). Pharisees were evidently a nonpresence in the sources the Evangelists had concerning the inquest, trial, and physical torture of Jesus. They make their first and only appearance before those events in the party that apprehended him in Gethsemane (John 18:3) and after that in joining chief priests and elders to ask Pilate to order the tomb secured to guard against theft of the body (Matt. 27:62-65). Pilate reportedly threw the problem back at them. The story may have been based on early explanations of the empty tomb as grave theft that had come to the attention of Jesus' disciples.

6. If there were a finding in modern scholarship of exclusive Roman responsibility for the activity against Jesus (apprehension, trial, execution), the tension in modern Christian–Jewish relations would not be much reduced by that fact. The "Sandmel principle" noted above remains undisturbed. Reduction of that tension must come from some other quarter.

7. The trial accounts that are set within the Passion narratives are a *post factum* dramatization calculated to present the death of Jesus as that of a just and innocent sufferer, and thereby to excite sympathy for him.[18] The historical opponents named in the Gospels are assumed by the authors to be the real ones. How much projection, confusion, and simple misinformation is at work is for the critical process to try to discover, just as that same process should be free to identify historical traditions that seem dependable. Overall, however, an eye should be kept on the apparent inclusion of details or briefer narratives for dramatic purposes. The Gospels were above all a homiletic, that is to say, a persuasive literature.

8. This study will proceed neither on the principle that the Gospel evidence on the trial is historically true unless proved false nor false unless proved true. It will proceed on the principle that it is *there*, and was placed there to say something in the realm of faith to the readers. The Gospels at the same time give the appearance of saying something to their readers in the realm of history. This study will assume that much, if not most, of that history is irrecoverable, but that as a parable for a truth deeper than that of mere history it is available. There will therefore be no hesitation in these pages to deal with statements in terms of their prima facie meaning which the writer is convinced is not historical. The meaning is theological.[19] If a given statement should in fact seem to be historical, well and good. Once one knows, however, that the Evangelists had other, deeper concerns (not unclouded by a certain search for

a scapegoat in what they were convinced was an injustice), one can be consistently on the lookout for that deeper meaning.

9. The method employed here will be ordinary historical method, which, when properly used, requires as much healthy skepticism in the trial of Jesus as in any human matter, coupled with a knowledge of the faith-based principles that underlay the composition of the Gospels.

10. Lastly, the present writer writes as a Christian. He has an interreligious and an irenic commitment, which he nonetheless hopes will keep him from misreading the evidence. As part of being a Christian, he is not committed to the guilt or innocence of any individuals, parties, or peoples in the sentencing of Jesus, least of all of people who are Jews. He has long been content that his faith does not depend on any such attributions, as it does not depend on a large quantity of data about Jesus beyond the fact that, after having taught the future certainty of God's reign, Jesus died and rose from the dead. He is convinced that a serious and dispassionate inquiry into the trial of Jesus from the Gospels and contemporary sources is capable of doing something—however little—to improve the climate of Christian–Jewish discourse. This is true if only because so much that has been written on the trial that is harmful to good relations is demonstrably false.

Chapter 2

WHAT ROMAN LAW ALLOWED

The Christians of Corinth were being invited by Paul in the middle fifties to exult in the cross of Christ.[1] Some in our day may think this a sublime response to the personal tragedy of the loss of Jesus. Nonetheless, the cross was a major embarrassment to Christians. To claim as king-messiah, "the worker of eschatological redemption," someone who had been crucified by the pagan Romans was not an easy matter. To say that he had been vindicated by God who raised him from the dead was to make a claim that provided more complication than relief. The Greeks found the notion of a second career in the body, such as they understood the Jews to mean, repulsive and grotesque, while the Jews of the Pharisee persuasion who believed in it for all or for the just had no category to handle the resurrection of a single individual before the general resurrection. Either way, it was not an easy gospel to proclaim.

The first Christians sought a solution in the way that came most natural to them as the Jewish group they largely were. They claimed that it had all happened by God's foreknowledge and decree, a claim, they said, which a careful reading of the Scriptures would bear out.[2] They further constructed in the Passion narratives midrashic accounts of the things that overtook their Lord in his last earthly days.[3]

All this was done in a context of history. The Jesus who died and rose was never claimed as a timeless figure but as someone who "suffered under Pontius Pilate," that is to say, within the years 26–36 of the Common Era. Luke speaks of a plot by the "scribes and chief priests" to hand Jesus over "to the office and authority of the governor" (20:19-20). He also gives the clearest statement of all the Evangelists of the charges against Jesus: "We found this man subverting our nation, opposing the payment of taxes to Caesar, and calling himself the Messiah, a king" (23:2). While the statement about a plot may well be interpretation, the two latter charges would constitute seditious behavior in the civil order. The First Epistle to Timothy has preserved the tradition of Jesus' testimony before the governor without interpretation: "Before . . . Christ Jesus, who in bearing witness made his noble profession before Pontius Pilate, I charge you . . ." (1 Tim. 6:13).

SOMETHING of the HISTORY
of ROMAN PALESTINE in the PERIOD

A few matters about the Jewish situation in Jesus' day are available from Roman sources, from the writings of the onetime Jewish general in the revolt, Josephus, retired to Rome as an imperial court historian (37/38–c. 101 CE), and from the Jewish religious philosopher of Alexandria, Philo (c. 13 BCE—45/50 CE). They include the information that Judaea was, from the year 6 CE onward, a province governed not by imperial legates of senatorial rank as was Syria, but by "knights" (*equites, hipparchoi*), men of equestrian rank. The first of these was Coponius, who was sent with "full powers, including capital punishment"[4] as Josephus says, or in another place, "to rule over the Jews with full authority."[5] His immediate superior was the legate to Syria, P. Sulpicius Quirinius, but Coponius evidently had large powers apart from him.

Pontius Pilate succeeded Valerius Gratus in the office of prefect of Judaea in 26. Where he was before that, we do not know. He takes his family name from the island due west of Naples called Pontia of the province of Campania. Pilate was an appointee of the emperor Tiberius whose adviser, Sejanus, pursued a strong anti-Jewish policy. Pilate seems to have tried to keep the peace, but his unyielding pro-Roman nationalism brought him into one adventure after another with the Jewish people.[6] Josephus mentions him in a reference to Jesus that may be genuine: "And, when Pilate had inflicted on him the punishment of the cross [on the indictment of our chief men . . .], those who had in the first place come to love him [Jesus] did not cease to."[7]

It is probable that the proper title of the office was *praefectus* before the time of the emperor Claudius (41–54 CE).[8] So, at least, Pilate is designated on a stone found at Caesarea in 1961:

> . . .] STIBERIEVM
> . . . PON] TIVSPILATVS
> . . . PRAEF] ECTVSIVDA [EA] E[9]

The stone was embedded in the landing of a flight of steps in an amphitheater, but it probably was originally the dedication of a building known as the "Tiberium" (perhaps a temple) which Pilate built at Caesarea while governor. Antonio Frova reconstructs the inscription to read: "Pontius Pilate, Prefect of Judaea [. . . has given?] Tiberium [to the Caesareans?]." The Latin inscription in Greek-speaking Caesarea is indicative of the imperial mentality.

Tacitus, writing at the end of the first century, uses the term *procurator,* which by then is proper to his time.[10] Matthew consistently refers to Pilate by the military-oriented title *hēgemōn* (rendered *praeses* by the Vulgate), while Mark and Luke in the parallel places simply designate him by name, as does John.[11] Luke uses *hēgemōn* once of Pilate at 20:20. The ordinary Greek equivalent of *procurator,* which is *epitropos,* does not occur in the Gospels to describe Pilate, although it is used in its basic sense of "foreman" or "steward" in other places.[12] *Praefectus* would normally be *eparchos* in Greek, a usage which the Synoptic Gospels do not have but which Josephus, writing later, does.[13]

WHAT CAN BE KNOWN of PILATE'S LEGAL POWERS

It may seem a needless exercise to establish that Pontius Pilate acted within his rights to hear the charges against Jesus and sentence him to death without further recourse. The considerations that follow are meant to show what a Roman prefect's juridical prerogatives were, so that the reader may determine whether the Evangelists wrote out of knowledge or ignorance of the imperial legal scheme.

Pilate as the prefect of a province possessed the full *imperium*, a term nowhere defined but described in its effects. These included criminal and political jurisdiction,[14] permanent military occupation, and the power to levy taxes.[15] Jurisdiction was personal from the emperor (*princeps*) and in capital sentences could not be delegated.[16] It is abundantly clear that both the earlier proconsuls and the later legates and prefects had power over the lives of Roman citizens. A fortiori, they had it over provincial subjects like Jesus. The only law that limited their power was the law against extortion. For the rest, they could do as they pleased.

The power that an official like Pilate had in criminal cases was called *coercitio* if it fell within the crimes listed in the statutes designated as public laws, for example, adultery, forgery, murder, bribery, and treason.[17] Anything that fell outside this order was dealt with by what was known as personal *cognitio*. The punishments inflicted under this scheme were *extra ordinem*.[18] Juries were not known in Roman trials whereas counselors were. There had to be a formulation of charges and penalties by the judge and a formal act of accusation.[19] The judgment could be handed down in chambers. The designated alternative, *pro tribunali* (a raised platform), is reflected in the Gospel account of Jesus' appearance before Pilate. This public situation is described by "on the judgment seat" of Matthew 27:19, *bēma* being the ordinary technical term for an official's raised platform or judicial bench.

Can we be sure that Pilate's situation was exactly as described above? There are small ambiguities, but in general such appears to be the pre-Claudian (i.e., prior to 41–54 CE) state of things. For Pilate to have enjoyed untrammeled *imperium*, his power as an equestrian governor of Judaea would have had to be the same as that of proconsuls and imperial legates. Josephus's two references to the powers of Coponius, new in his administrative post in Judaea in 6 CE, seem in context to be concerned not with the "right of the sword" over Roman citizens or conscripts in the army but the equivalent of the proconsular *imperium* in criminal and political matters.[20] Having troops under them, the prefects would need the power of discipline deriving from the *imperium* to be effective in the exercise of their military commands.

Sherwin-White points out the hazards of deducing too much from Josephus's accounts[21] of the insurrections Pilate quelled, not wishing to have any reader take Pilate's handling of crises as normative for day-to-day civil administration.[22] The classical Roman lawyers, with the possible exception of Callistratus, are silent on the powers of equestrian governors. Josephus's reference is probably to the criminal jurisdiction of prefect-governors, with the implication that such power is equal to that of other governors. Early evidence outside Josephus likewise indicates that the Judaean governors could do those things that imperial legates or proconsuls could do.[23] Tacitus is our chief source on the powers of the equestrian governors of Egypt (whose appointments resembled those of the administrators of various Alpine territories as well as of Sardinia and Judaea).[24] From Augustus's time onward, he says, "gradually elsewhere throughout the provinces and in the City other concessions were created that formerly were associated with the praetors only."[25] If "gradually"—*mox*—a large number of cases in other provinces and in Rome, which formerly fell under the cognizance of the magistrates, were transferred to the equestrian order, the full powers (*omne ius*) of Roman magistrates are those in question. Ulpian in *Ad edictum* refers to a "law" of the Roman people which gave powers to the Prefect of Egypt "similar to those of proconsuls."[26]

The PILATE of JEWISH HISTORY
versus the PILATE of the GOSPELS

We shall save for later an extended discussion of Pilate's right over Jesus' life—here simply assuming it—vis-à-vis the power of the Jewish people under Roman law over the lives of offenders against *their* Law. Something we can attend to immediately is the apparent glaring discrepancy between the character and conduct of Pilate as Philo and Josephus portray him and the account of his behavior found in the Gospels. It is true that Luke 13:1 reports an unspecified incident in which "some were present who told Jesus about the Galileans whose blood Pilate had mixed with their sacrifices."[27] The remainder of the portrayal of the Pilate of the Gospels is quite out of character, however, with this Lukan reference and with the description of him provided by Josephus and Philo, the latter quoting a letter of Agrippa I to Caligula.[28]

Josephus reported two of Pilate's brushes with Jewish religious sensibilities at length, plus an action against the Samaritans on Mount Gerizim which proved his undoing,[29] but did not append any judgment as to his character. Philo, on the other hand, accused him of "acts of corruption, insults, rapine, outrages on the people, arrogance, repeated murders of innocent victims, and constant and most galling savagery."[30] One might expect a similar, brief characterization of Pilate in the Gospels, where Herod the Great is the murderer of infants (Matt. 2:16) and the incestuous Herod Antipas is called "that fox" (Luke 13:32). A consideration, however, is the presumed need of the Christian communities for civil immunity, as a result of which the Gospel writers (John would be the exception, whose Jesus was made to challenge Pilate forcefully) may have avoided accusatory language against the Romans. The further presumption is that they experienced no similar scruple with respect to what survived of the Jewish royal house, the Herodians, the high priesthood, or Judaism's official teachers.

Whatever the causes at work, the Gospels portray Pilate as balanced and judicious, if somewhat vacillating, but in the end influenced by the desires of the mob. He listens to the representations of "the chief priests and the crowds" (Luke 23:4) and dialogues with Jesus over the charge that he claims to be a king (Matt. 27:11-14; Mark 15:2-5; Luke 23:2-5; in John 18:33-38 this brief exchange becomes a poetic disquisition by Jesus on kingship). Pilate finds no case against Jesus requiring the death sentence (Luke 23:4, 15) and bargains with the jealous chief priests (Mark 15:10) over the release of Barabbas in his stead (Matt. 27:15-26; Mark 15:6-15; Luke 23:18-25). Pilate's tone is legally conciliatory throughout, even if it is based on alleged hostile feelings toward the Jewish temple priesthood. Finally, Luke reports that, defeated in the bargaining, he "decreed that what they demanded should be done" (vv. 23, 24) and "delivered Jesus up to their wishes" (v. 25).

Some authors are convinced that the Gospel treatment of Pilate, as of the Passion accounts more generally, can be explained only by the influence upon collective communal traditions of a spirit of pleading with those in power. Paul Winter is such a one, who writes:

> In addition to the concern of early preachers to persuade Jews that the crucifixion proved Jesus to be the Elect of God expected of old, there enters a new motive . . . namely, the apologetic purpose of convincing Roman officials that the profession of the Christian faith was not subversive of imperial institutions.[31]

The fact of how Jesus died was well known, this scholar says, and was proving a serious obstacle to the propagation of Christianity throughout the empire. Hence the "descriptions of Pilate's actions at the trials of Jesus,"[32] so different from the portraits of the same man in Philo, Josephus, and Luke 13:1-2. Matthew in particular "displays a definite tendency to depict Pontius Pilate in a favourable light as a witness to Jesus' innocence."[33] Winter in making this deduction does not entertain any other motivation, for example, setting the pagan functionary in contrast with the highest religious authority in Israel, whose scandalous behavior was collaborating in the elimination of the man whom the Gospel writers thought to be the holiest if Jews and uniquely God's elect.

Brandon sees in Mark's account of Pilate a portrait of one not only incredibly weak but incredibly stupid. He was stupid because, according to Brandon, he would have had to report the amnesty or the conviction to Tiberius. But this necessity is something of which, as we have seen, we know nothing and must even presume otherwise. In the Markan account the governor resorts to a subterfuge in offering the chief priests the release of a popular resistance fighter (15:7-15) in order to save Jesus, "when he had himself the authority and the power to dismiss the charge."[34] As part of Brandon's conviction that Mark is accounting for Jesus' death (as an insurgent) to a Christian community at Rome, he is persuaded that, "having already represented Jesus as endorsing the Roman rule in Judaea by recognising the Jewish obligation to pay tribute to Caesar, Mark adroitly explained away the obvious problem of Jesus' execution for sedition against Rome."[35] He continues:

> That explanation was doubtless received with much gratitude and relief by the Christians in Rome, worried as they were by the evidence of the Jewish rebellion which they had recently witnessed in the imperial triumphal procession [i.e., that of Vespasian and his son Titus in the year 71, depicted on the Arch of Titus in the Roman Forum].[36]

For Brandon, Mark's dramatic narrative, with its reversal of the timorousness of the chief priests of Mark 11:32 and 14:1-2 to a swift and unlikely pressure demanding Jesus' death, served its purpose "for simple-minded readers."[37]

The question is whether the Gospel accounts of Pilate's conduct are so intrinsically impossible, from our knowledge of imperial juridical process, that the narrative elements must be branded a fabrication in their entirety. Many authors besides the above two are convinced of it. Note that the claim is not simply one of the accretion of legendary elements, like the dream of Pilate's wife in Matthew 27:19 and the petition of Joseph of Arimathea to Pilate asking for Jesus' body in Mark 15:43-46, pars. On this view, there can be nothing whatever historical about Pilate's reported conduct.

Obviously the answer to the puzzle must lie in the area of probability. The solution one chooses can only be deduced from what is more likely, even if at the end one makes the leap (as Winter and Brandon do) from what they consider likelihood to relative certainty.

It is one thing to say that an apologetic tendency seems to be at work. It is another to say that we have in the Gospel narratives of Pilate's conduct a thoroughgoing fiction. Apart from mention of the dream there is no question of the miraculous here. There is only the problem, well known to form critics, of a narrative shaped by theological and perhaps apologetic considerations. Are we compelled to say that Pilate could not have acted out of character on this occasion, hence that the developed story could not have had a historical tradition behind it? How rigorously must we maintain the impossibility of his resistance to Temple priestly pressure up to a point, following which expediency took over? What, in sum, is the probability that there was a historical tradition in Christian circles that Pilate not only sentenced Jesus to death but also took measures to withstand pressures to render such a sentence? We shall save an examination of the historical character of Pilate's reported conduct for later chapters on the individual Gospels.

A THOROUGHGOING HISTORICAL SKEPTICISM

Meanwhile, Bultmann is not inclined to admit any historicity to the Pilate narratives in the Synoptics or John. In the former case, this is part of his overall view that the "whole narrative in Mark is a secondary explanation of the brief statement in 15¹."[38] He is committed to a "*primitive narrative* which told very briefly of the arrest, the condemnation by the Sanhedrin and Pilate, the journey to the cross, the crucifixion and death."[39] All else was material developed from this tradition. "For the later Christian tradition, from which at all events this story [of an appearance before the high priest] comes, Jesus' Messianic claim, which was the chief issue between the Church and Judaism, could very well appear to be the ground of his condemnation."[40] Bultmann refuses to speculate on a historical substrate of the original trial before Pilate beyond supposing that the material in Mark 14:53*a* and perhaps 14:65 and 15:1-5 are echoes of an original, "in which *Jesus was taken away and sentenced.*"[41] The Barabbas episode has been inserted at Mark 15:6, displacing the end of the trial before Pilate. It ends with an account of Pilate's scourging of Jesus and handing him over to be crucified (Mark 15:15). In Bultmann's opinion, Luke may have in 22:66 an older version of Jesus before the Sanhedrin than that in Mark 15:1, but he has nothing more primitive for the trial before Pilate. Luke simply edits Mark, accounting for Pilate's action of condemnation by describing it as "principally governed by the feeling that the hierarchy would have had to advance a proper accusation against Jesus" (Luke 23:1-5, 13-25).[42] He thinks that the sending of Jesus from Pilate to Herod (23:6-16) is a legend developed out of Psalm 2:1 where the psalmist speaks of kings and princes in a plot against the LORD's anointed.

Dealing critically with the Fourth Gospel, Bultmann finds that the account there of Jesus before Pilate "offers a remarkable interweaving of tradition and specifically Johannine narration."[43] John is presumed to have employed and edited a source, a connected Passion story. It is "analogous to the Synoptic account . . . ; the Evangelist has cleverly set it forth and organised it through the repeated change of scenes."[44] Bultmann assigns John 18:30-37 and probably 38*a* to the Evangelist; 38*b*, 39-40; 19:1-3 and motifs in 19:13, 15, 16*a* to the source. He sees as John's theme the condemnation of Jesus by the "world," which is here represented by the Jewish authorities, while the Roman state lets him go free. "The truth is not rejected by the state as such [John 18:38], but by its representative."[45]

Bultmann presumably thinks that the Synoptic-like source of the Passion narrative used by John had some historical character but that this character was minimal and confined to the fact of Jesus' condemnation by Pilate, as in the Synoptics. The Evangelist "is not interested in whether Pilate really does let Barrabas [*sic*] go free, but he only shows how Pilate is led further down the slippery slope."[46] More generally, John's concern is not with what happens in history so much as with the antithesis between Jesus and the world. Paradoxically, the state's representative "can as well be open for God as for the world."[47]

While John's account of Jesus' appearance before Pilate can be faulted as history on many grounds, he has at least retained the correct name of the official residence (*praitōrion,* 18:33; cf. Acts 23:35, where another *praetorium* at Caesarea is mentioned) of the governor of a province. Holding back from entering a Gentile's dwelling to avoid ritual defilement is a detail that seems to ring true, although a purifying bath before this night's sundown, which in John's account marked the onset of Passover, could have eliminated it.[48] The behavior of Pilate in going out to the crowd is remarkably accommodating (v. 29) and their response to his inquiry about the charge, "If he were not a criminal, we would certainly not have handed him over to you," at least ill-advised in a group that was seeking cooperation in a judicial process. Pilate's suggestion in verse 31 that "the Jews" "take him and pass judgment on him according to your law" hardly seems like the action of a civil servant before whom a claimant to kingship has been brought.

This last phrase helps to cast doubt on the historical intent of John, whereas his theological intent is clear. The same is true of the addition of "to them" (19:16) to Mark's "he handed him over to be crucified." He wishes to convey the complicity of powerful forces against the innocent Jesus, and, if Bultmann is right, to identify paradoxically the Jewish leadership with "this world" and the Roman oppressor with the spirit of clemency. Yet John finally puts Pilate on the side of "this world" by describing him as "not of the truth" (18:38).

Improbabilities multiply, such as Pilate's leading Jesus out to the crowd after his mocking (19:4) and the injunction to a Jewish crowd to crucify him (v. 6), a mode of punishment the Jews did not use. Even if it were meant jeeringly, the Evangelist clearly uses it to place guilt on Jewish rather than Roman shoulders. *Lithostrōton* (19:13) normally means "paved with stones," although a mosaic inlay is a possible meaning.[49] The Evangelist does not identify

"*Gabbatha*" as if translating Stone Pavement into Hebrew, but merely says that it is so termed in Hebrew. The meaning of the Aramaic, transliterated form *Gabbatha* is not known, despite a variety of elaborate reconstructions. Josephus, a native Aramaic speaker, suggests "hill" for "Gabath."[50]

A final, possible echo of history is the phrase "friend of Caesar" (19:12) which, as mentioned above, has a history, first "friends of Augustus" in the early empire, later "*Philokaisar*" on the coins of Herod Agrippa I and in a reference of Philo to him.[51]

Josephus tells of a successor of Pilate, Gessius Florus, who (in the year 65) "took up his headquarters in [Herod's] Palace and on the next day had his tribunal (*bēma*) set before it."[52] This site seems without a pavement that would qualify for John's description, although it has never been fully excavated. In 1870 some huge stone slabs were uncovered on the East Hill immediately north of the temple precincts, leading some to accept a twelfth-century tradition that Pilate's judgment hall had been in this vicinity. Père L. H. Vincent excavated the site in the 1930s.[53] It is under the convent of Les Dames de Sion on the Via Dolorosa, where it is readily accessible, as is good archaeological information concerning it from the scholarly Sisters there.[54] The evidence from Josephus and Philo, on the other hand, favors Herod's Palace near the present Jaffa Gate (formerly on the West Hill) as the usual Jerusalem residence for the prefects.[55] Mark 15:16 uses *aulē*, not *praitōrion*. *Aulē* is Josephus's usual term for the palace that Herod built in 23 BCE. He never uses it to describe the fortress Antonia.[56]

In all of these speculations about Pilate and his exercise of power we intend to do no more than find points of contact, where they exist, between the traditions from which the four narratives of the trial were constructed and the Roman imperial presence in Jerusalem. We do this because Jesus certainly appeared before Pontius Pilate and was sentenced by him. It is not nearly so sure a matter that he appeared before Jewish religious authority in any judicial context. Whether he did so or not must be faced Gospel by Gospel.

And indeed, this must be our technique from this point on. Knowing what we do about the influence played by the presuppositions of each of the Evangelists in their work of proclaiming Jesus crucified and risen, we can examine the four trial accounts fruitfully only in terms of their four theological outlooks.

Chapter 3

The INTERROGATION and TRIAL according to MARK

Mark is all but universally acknowledged to have written the first of the four Gospels.[1] It is equally supposed that he worked from traditional materials. Most students of the Gospels hold that these materials were distinct, developed stories, even though minimally developed. For long it was thought that his sole gift was to string them together like pearls on a string; then his ingenuity as redactor (editor, collator) was acknowledged and he was credited as creator of a new literary form—"gospel." Only recently has the scholarly world discovered that his short if wordy Gospel in its articulated parts has the complexity of a Swiss watch. A minority holds the stories to have been already in gospel form. The theory of an existence of an Ur-Markus ("primitive Mark") has largely been abandoned.[2]

In determining which materials in Mark's Gospel bear the stamp of his authorship or final editorial hand, scholars are much more prone to say what the literary peculiarities of his composition are than to identify which of his materials derive from the tradition and what form they had there.[3] Examining a passage from the trial account in Mark (14:53—15:20) in terms of what Mark does with it is a far easier matter than hazarding a guess as to the previous layers of tradition from which it came. This has not kept numerous researchers from making the attempt, among them Ludger Schenke (1971), Lothar Ruppert (1972), Wolfgang Schenk (1974), and Detlev Dormeyer (1974).[4] The last named by means of vocabulary count and style-critical analysis arrives at a three-level situation of tradition and redaction for Mark 14:1—16:8. When the same account appears in some form in three Gospels or, as rarely happens, in four, the problem of the history of the tradition is far easier of solution as regards Matthew and Luke and occasionally John than in the case of Mark. With him it is never easy because he is the innovator. We cannot be entirely sure which of his materials are derivative and which he developed for his own purposes.

SOME THEORIES on MARK'S TARGET AUDIENCE

The chief clue to a Markan shaping of the tradition is provided by our knowledge of his theological concerns, paramount among them his depiction of Jesus as a just or innocent sufferer. About his apologetic or polemical interests we are less certain. To illustrate, Brandon takes it as axiomatic that Mark was written for a Roman Gentile community.[5] Now, that Mark had Gentile Christians in mind is fairly certain because of his preoccupation to show the transition of salvation from Jews who did not accept Jesus to Gentiles who did. But that his readership was a Roman community is far from clear. The second-century testimony of Papias that Mark reported Peter's teachings is seriously challenged by internal data (e.g., all the mentions of Peter could have come from the tradition, and there is no evidence of a knowledge of events at second hand through someone like Peter). The numerous Latin loanwords (e.g., *dēnarion, kentyriōn, kodrantēs, krabattos, legiōn,* and *spekoulatōr*) could have occurred anywhere in the empire that

Greek was spoken or, in some cases, Aramaic (Latin terms also became loanwords in Semitic languages). Much more likely than a Roman provenance for Mark is a Palestinian one, especially if the contrast between Galilean and Judaean Christian groups (Lohmeyer, Marxsen) is accepted as the setting for Mark's division of his materials. The division seems to occur between 1:14—7:23 (7:24—9:50 going with it as transition) and 10:1—16:8.

Despite Brandon's case made for the special significance of Jewish payment of tribute to Rome (Mark 12:13-17), the parenthetical references to "the abominable and destructive presence" or "the appalling sacrilege" (13:14) as Roman, and the statement "I am he" as a reference to Vespasian (13:6), it cannot be held with certainty that Mark was saying something by way of apologia to the Roman Christians or even to the imperial authorities. His engagement in polemic against the Jews who do not accept Jesus (3:22; 7:1; 8:15; 10:33; 14:10, 11, 43, 53; 15:11), along with his unfriendly references to scribes, Pharisees, Herod, and in the Passion narrative the high priest, chief priests, scribes, and elders, are much clearer matters.

There are those who hold that a major target of Mark is the Jerusalem community of Christians.[6] This would account, in the story of the entry into Jerusalem (11:1-19), for his downplaying of Davidic kingship and the Temple, both presumably favored by the Jerusalem Christians. It would even explain his unhappiness with Jesus' family and with Peter (3:21, 31-35; 5:37-43; 6:4; 8:33; 14:66-72), representative in Mark's day of leadership in the Jerusalem church.

While none of these polemical motifs is present beyond all doubt except that against the leadership of Judaism, the christological motifs of Mark are surely his great concern. His Gospel shows a consistent thrust forward through the Passion and resurrection to the parousia, during which the role of Jesus can be identified by the use Mark makes of titles. Perrin identifies five major sections of Mark's Gospel (1:16—3:6; 3:13—6:6*a*; 6:7—8:22; 8:27—10:45; 11:1—12:44), each of them concluding in a traditional Markan summary (3:7-12; 6:6*b*) or story (8:23-26; 10:46-52), except the last, which ends in the twofold climax of the apocalyptic discourse (13:5*b*—37) and the Passion narrative (14:13—16:8).[7] The fourth or central section (counting the last two as sections six and seven) contains the three Passion predictions (8:31; 9:31; 10:33-34) made in Caesarea Philippi (8:27), Galilee (9:30; Capernaum 9:33), and on the way up to Jerusalem (10:32). The first of these is linked by Mark redactionally to the transfiguration. Each of the three predictions is described as occasioning misunderstanding (8:32-33; 9:32; 10:35-41) and evoking Jesus' teaching on discipleship (8:34—9:1; 9:33-37; 10:42-45).

BELIEF in a SUFFERING SON of MAN RATHER THAN HISTORICAL CONCERN

The way Mark casts his trial narrative cannot be comprehended apart from the forward movement of the entire Gospel. He has been occupied throughout to identify Jesus as "Son of God" (1:1; 12:6; 15:39) and to interpret this title immediately in terms of "Son of Man." The titles "messiah" (8:29; 13:21) and "son of David" (11:10; 12:35) are robbed of any connotations of a restored royal line by Mark's putting them, respectively, in a context of a Son of Man who suffers rather than is victorious (8:31; 13:26), and who (11:2, 4, 7; cf. Matt. 21:1-11) rides humbly on an ass, as in Zechariah 9:9, rather than rules as a king. Mark possesses traditions on Jesus as a wonder-worker or "divine man" (not a Markan term), as evidenced by his use of them in 3:7-12, 5:22-42, and 7:24-35;[8] but he wishes to correct the false impression healings and exorcisms might give by providing a better Christology. He does this by challenging his readers to discipleship "in the context of the prospect of the coming of Jesus as Son of Man."[9] His polemic against a false Christology, as he conceives it, consists in subordinating the story of Jesus the wonder-worker to the Passion.

Mark stands in the early tradition of identifying the ministry of Jesus with the church to which Mark addresses himself, speaking of the one in terms of the other. Hence we do not look for any purely historical interest in Mark, understanding "history" as "an

interest in Jesus as he was in his earthly days." Such historical traditions as he may have at hand he puts in the service of a portrait of
the Jesus Christ who is someone to come as the victorious Son of
Man and who became such by way of ignominious suffering.

We have noted above in chapter 2 (see pp. 24–26) Bultmann's
contention that the entire Markan Passion narrative is the elabora-
tion of a primitive narrative of arrest, condemnation by the Sanhedrin and Pilate, journey to Calvary, and crucifixion and death.
This would confine the "trial" portions to 14:43—15:20. If, as seems
likely, the Gethsemane account (14:32-42) has been inserted by
Mark into an earlier narrative, verse 43 would pick up after verse
31. Mark uses in verse 43 as his familiar link "and immediately,"
coupled with a genitive absolute, "while he was still speaking." This
probably refers to Jesus' being at prayer in verse 35, although conceivably it could mean his rousing of his disciples in 41-42. Judas
is accompanied by a crowd (*ochlos,* v. 43), not the temple guard
of Luke (22:52) nor the soldiers/cohort and officer/tribune of John
(18:12 and guards/police of 18:3). The mob is armed, characteristically, with swords and clubs (v. 43). The detail is not nearly so
important as Mark's attribution of provocation, in the same verse, to
the "chief priests, the scribes, and the elders." This accords with his
designation of the plotters against Jesus in 14:1 (where the "elders"
do not occur, however) and 15:1, "the chief priests, with the elders
and scribes and the whole Sanhedrin." This is a fair description of
that body which was largely priestly but had its learned lawyers
(*grammateis*), possibly in the Pharisee tradition as holdovers from
the time of Queen Alexandra, 76–67 BCE, and lay elders as well.[10]

After betrayal by a kiss (14:45) comes the incident, probably
found in the tradition because also attested to by John 18:10-11,
of cutting off an ear of a servant of the high priest by one of those
standing by (v. 47); then Jesus' challenge to his captors in which he
declares himself no brigand (v. 48; *lēstēs,* i.e., highwayman, insur-
rectionist) but a teacher (v. 49). The details included have the ring
of novelistic embellishment.

There is only one important historical question. Was Jesus
apprehended at the initiative of certain of his fellow nationals

who had authority, as verse 43 states, or is the allegation simply a necessary consequence here in a Gospel that has religious authority pitted against him throughout? In other words, was the opposition by Jewish officialdom to those who believe in Jesus such in Mark's time—still a priestly Sanhedrin in the years 65–70—that he can conceive of the downfall of Jesus in no other way? Or is the primitive Passion account from which Mark seems to have worked the historical source for his mention of "chief priests, scribes, and elders"?[11]

The sequence of events in the Gospels, evidently dictated by a tradition so firm and dominant that none of the four Evangelists dared depart from it, is arrest, appearances before the chief priests and the governor, denial by Peter, crucifixion, and discovery of the empty tomb.[12] Many individual elements in these narratives are doubtless elaborations, but the main tradition is not readily challengeable. The primitive character of the Passion accounts is sufficient that we do not look for later free compositions in them which introduce opposition to Jesus from the Sanhedrin at the end of his life as the logical conclusion to earlier differences between him and priestly authority. If anything, matters would have gone in reverse, that is, a tension between Jesus and the priesthood earlier in his career would have been devised later to accord with the more primitive Passion narrative.

The ROLES of JUDAS, the SANHEDRIN, and the HIGH PRIEST

The Judas tradition, whatever the elements of his alleged motivation supplied by Matthew and John,[13] was one of complicity with religious leadership, not civil (Mark 14:43 rather than 15:1-2).

The virtual nonappearance of "Pharisees" in the Passion accounts supports the likelihood that Jesus' historical opponents were the priestly leaders as indicated.[14]

It is possible to maintain, of course, that the sole dependable traditional element, besides sentence at Pilate's hands, was the inscription (*titulus*) affixed to the cross (reported in four different wordings in Matt. 27:37, Mark 15:26, Luke 23:38, and John 19:19). Bultmann challenges this inscription, claiming it is the result of a progressive development from Mark 15:2 ("Are you the king of the Jews?") to 15:26 ("The king of the Jews"), then on to John 18:33-37, while Winter allows it, providing strong arguments for its historicity.[15] The common phrase in all four accounts is "the king of the Jews," which probably meant "of Judaea" in usage common at the time of describing a region by its people. One could hold that this piece of Roman ridicule, which resulted from a garbled view of Jewish messianism, came to be coupled with the church's later troubles over claims about Jesus which the pre-70 CE Sanhedrin called blasphemous. This conjunction of concerns in the mid-first century would then have yielded the "conspiracy theory" offered by the Gospels—namely, that of Jewish–Roman collaboration against Jesus—about his death.

Such a conclusion can only be arrived at, however, by setting aside a tradition of the antipathy of the priests that seems to be valid. Its appearance in Mark 14:10 and 14:43 is a doublet. The identification "Judas, one of the twelve" indicates that Mark retained it as he found it in two places, neither of which assumes the reader's familiarity with the preceding Gospel account (3:19). The element of plotting by the chief priests and scribes in 14:1 may well be overblown. Still, it is the tradition of the enmity of the Sanhedrin—clearest in 15:1—that accounts best for the presence of what is erroneously called the "Jewish trial" in Mark, in whatever form.

Much has been written on the areas of legal competence of the Sanhedrin under Rome and of its practice at the time of Jesus.[16] We can bypass lengthy discussion of the illegality of that court's procedures as reported in Mark if it can be shown that Mark possessed a tradition of a hearing by some priestly representatives which, for nonhistorical reasons (that is, his interpolation or "sandwich" technique), he situates at night.[17] The story of Peter's presence in the high priest's courtyard (14:54) and his threefold denial of Jesus (vv. 66-72) encloses the supposed interrogation of Jesus by "the chief priests and the whole council" (v. 55). His warming himself by firelight is the setting for what became a night trial in Mark's

narrative, possibly a metaphor for the light of Jesus without contrasted with the darkness of ignorance regarding him within.

Let us assume for the moment the traditional character of
15:1 (for reasons of the time of day, "daybreak" being credible as
an hour for doing serious business in that part of the world; for
its sobriety—with the phrase, "that is, the whole Council/Sanhe-
drin" constituting an exception; for the fact that 15:1 is in accord
with Luke 22:66a). On such supposition, Mark would have put the
other tradition which he had concerning a hearing (14:53-64) on
the previous night, in part because 15:1 contained the word *prōï*,
"very early." The other reason for locating the priestly hearing at
night has been mentioned, the device of inserting pericopes one
into one another, normally to highlight a relation between the
enclosed and the enclosures.[18]

Jesus has been arrested. A narrative is required to occupy him
until the resumption of activity early the next morning. Mark is
not at all deterred by the fact that his second of two sources has
the Sanhedrin reach the verdict the next morning—"all judged
him deserving of death" (14:64), but "very early they held a coun-
cil/consultation" or "reached a decision" (15:1). He possesses both
traditions and he means to use both. The one (14:53-64) is sand-
wiched between references to Peter's denial and becomes a night
trial. The other (15:1) is placed the next morning.

How much of a formal trial did Mark wish to portray before
Judaism's supreme council? It is doubtful that his tradition was
informed on either the actual facts in Jesus' case or the legal refine-
ments of a Jewish trial. Courts take testimony; therefore this one
did. The witnesses "did not agree" because any agreement of theirs
reached under the Law would have meant condemnation for Jesus
(cf. Deut. 19:15-21). But in Mark's eyes he was innocent. Therefore
those who testified did so "falsely" (14:56), probably in the sense
that for the Evangelist any testimony against Jesus was by definition false. Verses 55-56 and 57-59 look very much like two versions
of the same tradition. That the saying in verse 58, "I shall destroy
this temple, . . ." has a solid place in the tradition we know from
13:2 and 15:29 (cf. 11:17-18).[19] Mark may have as his reason for

calling the testimony false (concerning Jesus' saying that he would bring the temple down) that Jesus' disciples are still worshiping in it at the time he writes. The notion of a spiritual edifice, that is, one "not built with hands," occurs in 2 Corinthians 5:1 with reference to the heavenly bodies of the dead and Colossians 2:11 in a context of circumcision.[20] From these places we may conclude that there existed a convention of speech about an order of things that was God's doing rather than man's, "made by hands" being the ordinary biblical way to describe graven images and the idols made by pagans (cf. LXX Lev. 26:1, 30; Isa. 2:18; 21:9).

The climax of the passage is not Jesus' innocent silence before authority but his speech. Indeed, every indication is that the entire passage that describes Jesus' appearance before the high priest has been inserted by Mark as an epiphany or manifestation of him who has come as the Messiah and will come again as the Son of Man. For that reason we must spend some time analyzing Mark 14:61*b*-62.

The question the high priest puts is post-Easter in form, "Are you the Messiah, the Son of the Blessed One?" Interest in Jesus as Messiah may or may not have run high in his lifetime. The phrase "Son of the Blessed" is not, however, characteristically Jewish. It is a locution new in the community of believers in Christ's resurrection, so far as we can tell. Moreover, Jesus' reply, "I am" (softened by Matthew and the others in parallel places), coupled with what follows in verse 62, is meant to be a creedal affirmation of the Markan church. This is its whole reason for existence in his milieu. The two biblical passages alluded to in verse 62 are from Daniel and the book of Psalms. The question to be asked is, What does Mark mean to say by joining them in this fashion and putting them on Jesus' lips? Has he framed a prophecy of Jesus' exaltation after the crucifixion, or one of his future coming (*parousia*, "presence") in glory at the end? Or has he done both?

After Jesus' affirmation that he is both Messiah and Son of God, he is made by Mark to continue with a description of himself (14:62) by joining elements of Psalm 110:1 with Daniel 7:13. The same conjunction of texts occurs in Acts 7:56, helping to establish for us that it was part of Christian preaching to join them before either New Testament writer used them together. What is understood is the notion that Jesus by his resurrection has ascended to the glory of his Father ("Sit at my right hand," Ps. 110:1) as Son of Man—

> One like a son of man coming with the clouds of heaven;
> When he reached the Ancient One and was presented
>   before him,
> He received dominion, glory, and kingship. (Dan. 7:13f.)

In such a joining of the two texts there was added to the original understanding of Christ's resurrection, under the aspect of his glorification by his Father, the notion that Jesus had ascended to God as Son of Man.

The USE MARK MADE of DANIEL 7:13 and PSALM 110

Before proceeding further, we need to explore the origins of the phrases from the two Old Testament books to determine what use the church generally, and Mark in particular, was making of them. Psalm 110 can be dealt with first, as the simpler matter. It was a song in praise of a princely (110:3), hence a messianic, figure to whom Israel's God had given power at his enthronement. In doing so, the LORD (YHWH) had designated him his son from the dawning (v. 3). This royal figure possessed priestly power as well, not by way of Levitical descent but after the manner of the king-priest of ancient Salem, Melchizedek (v. 4). It is relatively easy to see how the early church would use this psalm in its preaching about Jesus, whom it thought to be king, priest, Son of God, and one who had been set over God's enemies by his resurrection; and, indeed, the church did so use it. It appears in a variety of places as testimony to the community's faith in the risen Christ (cf. Mark 12:36; Acts 2:34-35; Heb. 1:13; there are also numerous references to Jesus' standing or being seated "at the right hand of God": Rom. 8:34; Eph. 1:20; Col. 3:1).

But if the early occurrence of Psalm 110 in handbooks for preachers ("books of testimonies") is fairly certain,[21] the exact force assigned to Daniel 7:13 is not.[22] This verse occurs in a late-second-century BCE apocalyptic book which attempted to assure the partakers in the Maccabean uprising that their sufferings were not to be in vain but would be rewarded. The anonymous author of Daniel may have relied on an ancient myth found in Ugaritic and Tyrian sources in which the gods assemble to transmit power from one god ("Ancient of Days") to another younger god ("Son of man").[23] The poetic character of verses 7, 9-10, 13-14 indicates the existence of these verses prior to their use in the book of Daniel. The prophet-author interprets them in such a way that the son of man figure, in the kingship, dominion, and majesty that is given him, serves to reassure the survivors of the Maccabean martyrs that their dying shall not have been in vain.

In the vision of Daniel 7 a human figure comes after the four beasts and is set in contrast with them, as if to do God's work rather than engage in the power struggle of the empire. Ezekiel had used four living creatures in one of his visions, each with four faces, that of a man, a lion, an ox, and an eagle (1:5-11). The four beasts of Daniel's dream in chapter 7 (vv. 4-6) had been a lion, a bear, and a leopard—conventional motifs for Babylonia, Media, and Persia—while his fourth, the ten-horned beast (vv. 7-8), represented the ten kings of the Seleucid dynasty, and the "little horn" (v. 8) probably Antiochus IV Epiphanes (175–63 BCE). Israel's deliverer from all these predators was to be "one like a son of man" (v. 13). His humanity—probably derived from Ezekiel's usage—was symbolic, but what it stood for was divine deliverance. Some mysterious figure was required to give the readers assurance that God would intervene in behalf of "the holy ones of the Most High" (v. 27). The deepest meaning of the vision was that kingship, dominion, and majesty, under the LORD, should be theirs.

But the imagery of the book of Daniel underwent a certain transition. Two subsequent writers employed the language of Daniel 7 to make the manlike figure central in a way that he had not been in that apocalyptic vision. The writings in question were the postbiblical books of *1* (Ethiopic) *Enoch* and *4 Ezra*. *1 Enoch* took its rise from Genesis 5:24, which said of Enoch, Methuselah's father, that "he walked with God and was no longer here, for God took him." A whole Enoch saga was developed in which his spirit was carried off "on the chariots of the spirit" (*1 Enoch* 70:2), ascending into the heavens where he saw "the holy sons of God" (71:1). There are extensive borrowings from Ezekiel 1 and Daniel 7 in these two chapters, references to flaming cherubim, streams of fire, and to God as the "Head of Days":

> His head white and pure as wool,
> And His raiment indescribable. (71:10; cf. 47:3)

The important detail in this book is that Enoch himself is addressed as the son of man. The link is that he was carried off to the heights, an occurrence interpreted in terms of Daniel 7:13: "And he [the angel Michael] translated my spirit into the heaven of heavens. . . . And my spirit was transfigured. . . . And he came to me and greeted me . . . and said . . . : 'You are the Son of man who is born unto justice. . . . He proclaims to you peace in the name of the world to come. . . . And all shall walk in your ways since justice never forsakes you. . . . And they shall not be separated from you for ever and ever'" (71:5, 11, 14, 15, 16, 17). The visionary author, in other words, is called to look upon Enoch summoned to heaven where, in the company of Michael and Raphael, Gabriel and Phanuel, he has become the Son of man.

Chapters 70–71 seem to be the earliest written of the three descriptions of the call of Enoch, 14:8-25 and 60:1-6 being the other two.[24] In all of them, God (or the "Great Glory" as he is called in 14:20) presides over an angelic court. The seer who writes the book is addressed as "You son of man" in 60:10. In 71:14-17 alone of the three "calls" the Son of man appears. There he is a righteous figure distinct from the seer. The most complete description of this Son of man is found in 69:26-29 at the close of the third similitude.[25] He sits on the throne of his glory and has the sum of judgment given to him (v. 27); all evil shall pass away before his face (v.

29); his word shall go forth and be strong before the Lord of Spirits (ibid.). The seer has taken the scene from Daniel 7 and altered it thoroughly. There, the "one like a son of man" is presented before the Ancient One to receive dominion (vv. 13-14). In *Enoch*, the son of man figure becomes the end-time judge. What is important about him is the judgment he exercises from the throne of God on which he sits (69:27, 29).

Still another work of Jewish apocalyptic that employs the son of man concept from Daniel 7 and that needs to be mentioned is *4 Ezra* (*II Esdras*; late first century, according to B. M. Metzger in Charlesworth) where in chapter 13 a vision is reported of a "man coming up from the heart of the sea" (v. 25). He is called "my Son," and hence is a messianic figure (v. 37). He will function as a deliverer in a spirit of peace (vv. 29-31). Of him it is said that "this Man [from the sea] flew with the clouds of heaven" (v. 3). In Daniel 7:13 the clouds were something that the one like a son of man came "with." They are merely background for the scene. In *4 Ezra* they characterize his movement, his coming in glory. This passage is the first usage in Jewish apocalyptic that links the clouds with the movement of the figure. In it, of course, he does not come from heaven to earth; the scene is purely heavenly. But the operative phrase is the one that says he flew "with the clouds."

JESUS' CONFESSION before the HIGH PRIEST and the CHURCH'S END-TIME FAITH

Verse 14:62 of Mark is the second place in this Gospel where the Daniel 7 passage is employed. The first is 13:26. There had been earlier references in Mark to Jesus' exaltation (8:38; 9:2-8; 10:37), all of them speaking of it as a future event. Every indication is that in these five passages Mark viewed it as future, even at the time of his writing. Chapter 13 contains Mark's one apocalypse. He has been speaking of trials of every sort (v. 24) and the falling of stars from the skies (v. 25). Then, he says, "men [literally, they] will see 'the Son of man coming in the clouds' with great power and glory. He will dispatch his angels and assemble his chosen from the four winds, from the farthest bounds of earth and sky" (13:26-27). Mark here uses Daniel 7:13 in much the way it occurs in its context, namely, to describe the acceptance of dominion by one like a son of man. Many see in this passage a Markan reference to the parousia because of the phrase "coming in clouds"; cf. Matthew 26:64, *on* clouds. The supposition is that the Evangelist Mark is describing the descent of the Son of Man to earth to judge it at the end of time.

It is possible, however, that in 13:26 Mark means to describe the exaltation of Jesus, that is, his enthronement after resurrection, and only turns to the parousia in verse 27. One indication of this would be the shaking of the heavenly hosts in verse 25, a defeat of the spirit world that is concomitant with Jesus' enthronement in several New Testament hymns. Once defeated, the fallen powers will see the Son of Man coming in power and glory (13:26).[26] Then the chosen will be summoned by the enthroned Lord, through the ministry of angels, to be with him (v. 27). The movement of Jesus in verse 26 is upward. It is his progress toward dominion and kingship.

Matthew (24:29-31) and Luke (21:25-28) independently change the character of the Markan description. The two Evangelists turn a Markan ascent to enthronement, respectively, into a "Matthean descent to the earth" and a Lukan description of "the dissolution of the heavens and the earth and . . . the dire plight of angels and men."[27]

It is not to be taken as certain that Mark 13:26 describes the ascent of Christ to glory on high, although it does seem probable. The point is, it is even less certain that the verse describes his return at the end of days.[28] Of indisputable importance is the fact that the apocalyptic literature of late Judaism does not seem to have produced any sayings like Mark 13:26 in which a heavenly Son of man comes in clouds. The passage that is closest, *4 Ezra* 13:3, "this Man flew with clouds of heaven," sends him up from the sea to the top of a great mountain. Clearly this is not a development of Daniel 7:13 like that of Mark 13:26 and 14:62.

The first of these Markan passages, 13:26, prepares us for the second, the saying of Jesus in response to the high priest, 14:62.

Before we proceed to it, we should observe Mark's basic view of Jesus' exaltation. For him it was the first event in a process that would conclude in the parousia. The end time was inaugurated by it, but the Palestinian- or Syrian-based community with which Mark is concerned has as its vocation the enduring of suffering and persecution before the final consummation. Jesus will return in glory and power, it is true, but in his absence believers have to content themselves with the gift of the Holy Spirit. Mark 13:11 is a good example of this: when they arrest you, do not worry about what to say; "Speak what is given to you at that hour; it is not you who speak but the holy Spirit."

When Luke comes to describe the gift of the Spirit at work (21:15), he connects it with the activity of Jesus as Lord ("*I* shall give you mouth and wisdom"), something that Mark never does. The earliest Palestinian church did not think that its Lord would be long in coming. Hence Mark could describe Jesus' enthronement in one verse and his return to judge in the next, as in 13:26-27 above.

As the time between his departure and return grew longer, however, there was the need to account for his role and activity during the interim. (See Acts 3:20, 21*a,* about "the Christ appointed for you, Jesus," whom God will send, "whom it is necessary for heaven to receive until the 'times of restoration for all things.'") This would explain the use made by the early Christians of Psalm 110:1. This verse, in accommodated form, saw Jesus already exalted and active in the life of the church. By the time of Mark 14:62, the two verses from Psalm 110 and Daniel 7 have already been joined. Their unification *may* be Mark's work; it certainly reflects his Christology and his eschatology. But since the linking ties Jesus' enthronement with the parousia event it can be more primitive still, the work of Palestinian communities in which the members looked on Jesus' kingly dominion as future. The church was suffering now. It would be vindicated later. This is what the two biblical verses in conjunction affirm.

This view is supported by the fact that Mark 14:61-62 suggests an eschatological setting for Psalm 110:1, the only place in the New Testament where this is done. By putting this verse and Daniel

7:13 together, the earliest community was fixing Jesus' enthronement in a context of the parousia event.[29] Norman Perrin's view is
neater than this, namely, that "Jesus must first be regarded as having ascended to heaven as the Son of man [previous to his seating]
before he can 'come with the clouds' from heaven as that Son of
man."[30] Neither position, however, is absolutely required in order
to make sense of the creedal affirmation of the Markan church
represented by the exchange between the high priest and Jesus.
Whichever stand one takes on Jesus' ascent and descent, it is clear
that the verses are included at this point as the penultimate Markan statement of Jesus' saving role. The last will come in 16:6-7:
"He has been raised up; he is not here. . . . He is going ahead of you
into Galilee, where you will see him just as he told you."

CHALLENGE and RESPONSE:
MARK'S FAITH in WHO JESUS IS

The high priest is never named in Mark. In his question, "Are you
the Messiah, the Son of the Blessed One?" (14:61), he voices the
chief difference between the emerging Rabbinic-period Judaism and the nascent church: the claim of Jesus' messianic status.
Since this was the issue between them, the church would naturally
think it the most probable reason for Jesus' condemnation. The
high priest's first two brief questions to Jesus (v. 60), asking why
he does not answer and what the testimony against him means,
do not follow logically upon the false and conflicting testimony
reported in verses 57-59. Bultmann thinks the latter secondary,
the trial story having been framed in the first instance to record
the conviction of Christians that Jesus was condemned for claiming to be the Messiah.[31]

As the high priest puts the question in verse 61, the "you" is
emphatic because unusual. Uncommon, too, is "Son of the Blessed,"
a euphemistic avoidance of the divine name. Matthew, perhaps ill
at ease with it because he was more used to "the Holy One, blessed
be he,"[32] changes it to the "Son of God" (26:63). This is not a Jewish title for the Messiah, but by Matthew's time it had become a

Christian one. Jesus' failure to respond is probably compounded of Isaiah 53:7 ("He opened not his mouth") and the stance of the Markan church in the face of testimony which it considered false. It is this church to which the next question ("once again," 61*b*) is being put and which then gives the answer attributed to Jesus. He responds first with a direct "yes" ("I am") so as to place the church's faith in his future eschatological glorification ("and you will see")[33] beyond doubt. The first part of Jesus' answer combines the Danielic son of man with the seating of a kingly figure at the right hand of God (the pious circumlocution "the Power" serving as an authentic touch). The second part describes the coming of such a one with the clouds of heaven.

In general the claim is being made for Jesus, in words ascribed to him, that the glorious destiny reserved for the Messiah will be seen to be his. The main emphasis of the first part of the answer is on triumphal enthronement; of the second part, on manifestation at the end. If Daniel 7:13 was used in the primitive church for both ascension and parousia traditions, this would explain its ambivalent use here. Perrin posits, in the already existing tradition, the joining of Daniel 7:13 and Psalm 110:1 to account for "the Son of man seated at the right hand of the Power." A second tradition, joining Daniel 7:13 to Zechariah 12:10-11 (where an "only son" and a "firstborn" is "thrust through," then looked upon in grief and mourning), would account for "the Son of man coming with the clouds of heaven."

Jesus' response to the high priest is, therefore, clearly to be understood as part of Mark's theology. Jesus has been taken away; he is no longer with his church. It is the lot of his followers to suffer and wait. But at God's appointed time, at the end, they will see him: risen, glorified, made manifest. Mark 13:26 and 14:62, the latter in both of its phrases, combine to support the idea that eschatological glorification lies ahead for Jesus. Mark tells of the resurrection mystery in his last brief chapter (eight verses) in the same vein. There, no one actually sees Jesus glorified. They learn that he has been raised up and taken away (16:6), and are directed to Galilee, where, at some future (eschatological?) time, they are told: "You will see him" (v. 7).

The CHARGE of BLASPHEMY

Mark has been much criticized for his ignorance of Jewish customs when, in 14:63 and 64, he has the high priest tear his clothing and declare that what he has just heard is blasphemy.[34] Obviously, the claim to messiahship was not blasphemous. Many had made it before, and Bar Kokhba would make it subsequently. Invoking the divine name insultingly was the essence of blasphemous speech and, as Mark reports matters, it did not occur. The later Christian understanding of "messiah" and "son of God" accounts for Mark's use of the term here, an indication that in polemical exchange the claims made for a man impugned the sovereign majesty of God. The detail of rending one's garments in horror had progressed from King Hezekiah's time (2 Kings 18:37; 19:1) to the point where the practice is described as the stylized behavior of judges in the Mishnah (*Sanhedrin* 7.5). As a sign of resistance to impious utterance, therefore, it was certainly well known.

The question before us, we cannot repeat too strongly, is not one of what took place between Jesus and the high priest on a certain night. Any such confrontation is of doubtful historicity. The question is, rather, What had the Markan community's experience been with the highest religious authority in Judaism over claims made for the man Jesus? So far as Mark knows, the claims that he summarizes as faith statements in verses 61-62 have been received as blasphemous. Condemnations are being issued in his day without the summoning of witnesses. However Christians are being dealt with (and we have some indications in 6:8-11; 8:14-18; 13:11-13), it is at least clear to Mark that the Jesus of whom messianic claims were being made had died as a result in good part of official opposition by the Temple priestly community.

Mark has the high priest ask his peers how things appear to them upon hearing "the blasphemy" (14:64). They all adjudge him worthy of death (v. 64). Valiant efforts have been made to declare this the language of an inquest, not a trial, and the judgment rendered an opinion, not a verdict. Such efforts are, in a sense, time lost. So far as Mark is concerned, the supreme council of the people

Israel had acted effectively to bring about Jesus' death. He knows how his Master ended. He likewise knows a tradition of an inimical stance which he presumes to have been identical with that of his own day. The Evangelist puts two and two together and arrives at twenty-two: he creates a "trial" where one had not existed.[35]

If the details in sum are historically doubtful, is it not then the case that any opposition between the Sanhedrin and Jesus must be called in question? Paul Winter thinks that while Mark 15:1 is based on a written tradition, "the high-priest and his staff played only a minor part in bringing Jesus to trial before Pilate."[36] He argues that all the data provided by Mark concerning the grounds for Jesus' arrest (14:48*b*), the formal accusation (15:2), and the death sentence (15:26) are based on dependable tradition because they form a coherent whole and are in the political order. This certainly cannot be denied. Nonetheless, its truth does not rule out the dependability of some tradition of hostility to Jesus on religious grounds (14:49*a*; 15:1*a*; 31-32*a*). The fact that Mark has, for theological reasons, made an insertion about a religious inquiry (14:55-64) causes Winter to say that he has woven the tale out of whole cloth. In this we agree with him. But the echoes of an ideological opposition going back to Jesus' lifetime are not so readily stilled as Winter's attempt to minimize them would have it.[37] They survive in the Gospels, and they seem to be there for historical reasons.

JESUS MOCKED, BETRAYED

Allowing some measure of historicity to Mark 14:65, in which Jesus is manhandled and urged to prophesy, is almost universal among the critics. Bultmann thinks that Mark's placing it here is unfortunate and that in an older tradition that Luke (22:63-65) had, although he had no trial source, it followed Jesus' arrest—the order retained by Luke.[38] He does not think that it (or Luke 22:63) is a doublet of Mark 15:16-20*a*, where the soldiers mock Jesus.[39] The latter passage is, for Bultmann, probably an insertion which expands the "after he had had Jesus scourged" (*phragellōsas*) of 15:15*b*.[40]

Winter likewise grants the independence of Luke 22:63-65, from which Mark is developed.[41] This leads D. R. Catchpole to accuse all those like Winter who consider everything from Mark 14:53*b* to 65 to be an insertion of inconsistency. "Recognizing therefore the existence of an earlier tradition behind the Markan version of the mockery," he writes, "the same approach must be adopted towards the accompanying version of the trial."[42] The statement is true if correctly understood. The chief difference between Catchpole and the present writer is that the historicity of the trial tradition for him means a formal hearing of some sort, whereas for this writer any summoning of Jesus before any priestly figure or figures will satisfy the demands of what actually took place. No more than this is necessary to account for the theological development of the two different sources that underlay Mark and Luke–John.

The theme of mockery of Jesus occurs in Mark at 14:65 (as a prophet, by certain members of the Sanhedrin); at 15:16-20 (as a king, by Roman soldiers); and at 15:29-32 (as the rebuilder of the Temple, by passersby; also by chief priests and scribes and those crucified with him). Undoubtedly certain biblical passages were influential in the creation of this motif, in particular Psalms 22:7-8; 69:10-13; Isaiah 50:6; 53:3; Wisdom 2:16-20. Loisy thought that Jesus was crucified as a mock king in a pagan carnival ritual,[43] while Gunnar Rudberg pointed to a Hellenistic custom of mocking slaves (*ZNW*, 1925) and W. C. van Unnik later in the same journal (1930) speculated that there was some custom of a game behind it. The challenge to "play the prophet" is the relatively simple one of asking Jesus to tell who hit him, as is done in children's games. The officers of 65*b* are presumably those of the high priest, although historicity need not concern us here. It does not concern one commentator who thinks that Mark is in the narrative world and has Jesus return the mockery with "Am I?"[44] In his reading of "the war of myths" the Jewish court has condemned Jesus.[45]

Mark 14:66-72, Peter's denial, is the completion of the narrative begun in verses 53-54 and the fulfillment of Jesus' prophecy in 30-31. The story of the denial doubtless occurred after verse 52 in an earlier version, the position it has in Luke (22:54-62). Bultmann calls the story of Peter "legendary and literary"[46] and thinks that Luke 22:31-32 ("Simon! Simon! Remember that Satan has asked for you . . .") shows that the legend of the betrayal did not always belong to the Passion story. The servant girl's designation of Jesus in Mark 14:67 as a Nazarene followed by his proper name is both contemptuous and a possible indication of the ordinary way Jesus and his followers were spoken of at this early date (i.e., as *Notzrim*, "Nazarenes"—later a Hebrew designation for Christians). Peter's initial response, meant to be a denial, is confused in its wording (v. 68). In the Greek it bears a resemblance to the form of an oath used by the rabbis. Peter's cursing in verse 71 is not to be confused with his swearing, that is, denial under solemn oath, in the same verse. This is the third of the predicted three denials, the second having occurred in verse 70. A second cockcrow follows (v. 72), thereby fulfilling Jesus' earlier prophecy (14:30-31).

MARK'S SETTING of TIMES and PLACES; The BARABBAS STORY

Burkill calls attention to the construction of the remainder of the Passion narrative which, he says, is in five parts (15:1-20; 21-32; 33-41; 42-47; 16:1-8).[47] Each is marked by some notice of time, thus 15:1, "daybreak"; 15:25, "about nine in the morning"; 15:33, darkness over the countryside between "noon" and "mid-afternoon," shortly after which Jesus "breathed his last," verse 37; 15:42, "as it grew dark," the burial of Jesus; and 16:2, "very early, just after sunrise, on the first day of the week." The first two, plus the preceding 14:53-72, contain notice of change of place (14:53, from Gethsemane to the high priest; 15:1, from the high priest's court to Pilate; 15:21-22, from Pilate's court to Golgotha). In all three of those sections (14:53-72; 15:1-20; 15:21-32) Jesus is subjected to mockery (see opening sentence, two paragraphs above this one).

A second triad that follows this contains accounts of the apostolic kerygma of 1 Corinthians 15:3-4, where it is said Jesus "died, . . . was buried, . . . and rose on the third day": 15:33-41 (death); 42-47 (burial); 16:1-8 (resurrection). Mark adds the division into three-hour intervals (the Roman military "watches") as a similar grouping (cf. 15:25; 33); likewise the three classes of mockers (15:29-32) and the three women named in 15:40. Even if not every detail is intended, the Evangelist surely employs groups of three in the Passion narrative as he does elsewhere. The technique he is employing of contrast between innocence and guilt, between moral strength and weakness, is undeniable.

The Barabbas story (15:6-15a) provides as much clear evidence of Mark's narrative technique, perhaps, as does his intercalation of the "night trial" between portions of Peter's denial. It betrays at verse 12 an interest consistent with verses 2 and 26 in Jesus as "king of the Jews/ Judaea." It is, in fact, an expansion concerned with that title. While a jailed rebel (v. 7) goes free, the sovereign who, like Israel's LORD, is its only king for Mark, is sentenced to death. Mark speaks of "the uprising" (v. 7) as if everybody knew about it, even though we cannot identify it from other sources. Barabbas's name means "son of the father" in Aramaic, an epithet by which certain rabbis are known in the Talmud in conjunction with given names. Certain manuscripts of Matthew have "Jesus Barabbas" (27:16-17), but this is more likely to represent a copyist's lively sense of contrast than any historical tradition.

The larger question is, Does the Barabbas tale represent any historical tradition whatever? It is not easy to say. The silence of Roman and Jewish sources on any such Passover tradition of amnesty tells against it. There was in the ancient world, it is true, the practice of *abolitio* or suspension of a suit by authority, not to speak of the reference in one papyrus to the action of the governor of Egypt quite like that of Pilate.[48] There is nothing to hinder the possibility that a historical incident like this one was joined to the church's tradition on Jesus' condemnation. The appearance of a particular name, Barabbas, favors historicity. Again, it could have been a legendary feature from the beginning (rooted in the Christian claim that Jesus was Son of the Father?). This is an instance of a Gospel story, the theological intent of which is clear, but about which nothing certain can be said beyond the fact of legendary development. As it appears, it is inserted into Pilate's formal interrogation as a means of highlighting his will to set Jesus free. It is highly unlikely that Pilate would have released a man guilty of crimes like murder and sedition (15:7). The contrast between Barabbas's condition and Jesus' is very clear to Mark. The historical question is, Could the irony of such a situation have suggested itself to Pilate as well?

The UNAVAILABILITY of CLEAR ANSWERS to CLEARLY POSED QUESTIONS

The whole effort of the present chapter has been to avoid raising those historical questions for which Mark's Gospel provides no dependable answers and to look into those theological and apologetic questions for which it does. It is no service to the Gospels to return constantly to their historical character when it seems quite clear that such was a matter of small interest to their authors. On the other hand, it is fair to point out the details that seem irreducibly factual so as to provide the freedom to discuss what Mark was really at pains to show.

Those details in the Markan trial before Pilate seem to be two. They occur in verses 15:10 and 15:15. Both use forms of the verb *paradidōmi*, the "chief priests handed him over" to Pilate in the first instance, Pilate to the executioners in the second. We know that something like this must have taken place, whoever Mark's "chief priests" were. It is a certain matter that Pilate, after sentencing Jesus (the most basic historical datum, but missing from Mark's account), committed him to the military arm for crucifixion. Verse 1*a* affirms that the "they" of verse 1*b* was the priestly leadership. As the sentence stands, it is a link joining what went before with what follows, a means to get Jesus before imperial authority and onto the cross. To reclassify it as an apologetic or a polemical fiction would require evidence that we do not possess, namely, some indication of the actual group responsible for bringing him before imperial authority, if there were any other than the Temple priestly leadership itself.

One may theorize that the operation was a civil one from first to last, some private informant or informants having acted as promoters of a charge against Jesus of armed revolt. But for that theory to hold up there is the necessity of suppressing all the Gospel evidence of religious opposition to him (e.g., Mark 15:10-11) and putting in its place an active civil concern for his activities.

Such is the theory of the conspiracy of the Christian community against a truthful report because the movement had changed from violent to peaceful in character shortly after Jesus' death. The historical fragments of the sequence Gethsemane—priesthood—imperial court—execution are, however, simply there. The subsequent exacerbation of Christian relationships with Jewish authority may very well account for the form of the various Gospel accounts. It cannot account so readily for their substance. An oligarchy in Jesus' lifetime indifferent to the impact he was making on the people is far less credible than one that was not, one that merely stood by while the governor conveniently relieved it of the man who was its great embarrassment.

It serves no useful purpose to argue theoretically whether Pilate, that firm-willed despot, could have been influenced by the irony of Jesus' situation vis-à-vis the priestly leadership, still less whether he was attracted by Jesus' personality. Neither is it important to ask whether the case of this exceptional prisoner might not have been marked by all kinds of exceptions, both of juridical procedure and uncharacteristic moves for clemency on Pilate's part. To all such questions the answer is, it may well have been.

Undoubtedly the last days of the unique figure Jesus were unique. They are certainly reported as such in the only records we have. That is not the problem, however. The problem is, Does the overwhelming evidence of a theological concern on Mark's part—and a commitment to Jesus as "divine man" by those who seem to have produced a story cycle before him—permit us to argue for the full historicity of the various narratives in the Passion account? If not, why then should we care about something that it is doubtful Mark cared about? The oldest sin in scholarship is to impose questions on the past in which it was not interested.

Mark was concerned to proclaim that the man who stood before the supreme religious authority was the one who would ascend victoriously in the future, fully vindicated, as the executor of eschatological judgment (13:26; 14:62). He had to affirm in the face of that still potent authority the very claim it was daily occupied in denying. Moreover, he had to describe some confrontation between Jesus and the supreme civil authority that would spell out the meaning of the title on the cross (15:26). This, too, he did—possibly with the aid of an already developed narrative—making Jesus react in both cases to the accusations against him in silence (14:61; 15:5). The detail of a scourging (15:15) may be the one historical tradition remaining in an account that is otherwise theological in its concern: innocent silence before the clear expression of the power of "this world." In such case, the imperial functionary might at least have had the wisdom to show some hesitation at the phenomenon of the numinous in the form of a man. Mark makes the point that the religious functionary was incapable of it.

To recapitulate, then, the history of the tradition on the trial sequence in Mark: the arrest account (14:43-50), before it contained its present elaborations, was probably followed by a description of Jesus' having been apprehended (14:51a; possibly also 65) and sentenced (15:1-5). However the account of the trial before Pilate might at one time have ended, the Barabbas incident was inserted, leaving only 15:15b from the original. The narrative elements would then have included 20b-24a and perhaps 27 and 37. "All these items are not stories as such, but an historical narrative that is told in short statements."[49]

Mark's motivating concerns place in doubt who gave the command for Jesus' arrest. The armed mob in the garden is described as sent by "the chief priests, the scribes, and the elders" (14:43b), but the actual authorization of the apprehenders remains unclear. Similarly unresolved in Mark is the speed of the settlement as between Jewish and Roman authorities. It is evident that he means to implicate both. The swiftness of the death sentence, however, even if Mark's chronology is historically undependable,[50] argues to some kind of previous collaboration between the religious authorities and Pilate. This is not on the face of it unthinkable, since we know that the high priests held office by Roman sufferance[51] and that the interplay between these two powers was constant. From a purely historical standpoint it is impossible to place the blame for Jesus' death squarely on the shoulders of any particular group. This is largely because Mark is interested in implicating persons of bad will without special regard to their religious or political allegiance.

He ends with a coalition of Jewish authorities and Rome, the former concerned with proper observance of the law and temple ritual, the latter with a subject people in revolt and claims to king-ship. Jesus' teaching on freedom from the law as it was currently beginning to be interpreted, and his claims for the sovereign rule of his Father only, could easily have brought the two powers together in a coincidence of interest.

Mark paints the priestly leaders (whom he has acting in concert as "the Sanhedrin") as aggressive, Pilate as diffident. His selection of details and his emphasis were probably for purposes of alerting his readership to the situation in his own day. Whatever the case, Mark's choices were influential on Matthew and, through him, on all Christian generations since. The Lukan and Johannine Passion sources, more dependable historically in several matters as we shall see, seem to have been soberer and less dramatized accounts of the same events. If the latter two Gospels alone existed, the story of Christian–Jewish relations might be somewhat improved in the matter of the trial, but probably unaltered overall.

Chapter 4

The HISTORY of the TRADITION of the INTERROGATION and TRIAL in MATTHEW

The Gospel according to Mark seems to be interested in modifying and correcting the view found in a prior source (the cycles of miracle stories), even while accepting it, that Jesus was a heavenly man. This the author does by an editorial technique which stresses at every point that the suffering Son of Man, a hidden figure, is none other than the Son of God. Jesus is revealed as such, after the crucifixion, by the epiphany of a risen life which is made manifest in Galilee (or, as some would have it, of a parousia to be made manifest in Galilee).

St. Matthew's Gospel, on the other hand, is interested in showing that everything that happens to Jesus is part of a divine decree. Nothing comes about by chance but will happen at "my appointed time" (26:18). The operative word in Matthew is *dei,* "it must be."

The first instance of Jesus' majesty as the Son of God in the Matthew Passion narrative occurs at the time of his arrest. He can call on his Father, who will "provide at a moment's notice more than twelve legions of angels" (26:53; the detail is missing from Mark and Luke). Jesus does not because his suffering is voluntary and obedient. When Matthew alters Mark—to whom in general he stays faithful in the specifically trial portions—he does so to heighten the event as an action of God. It is always the Son of God who suffers and dies in Matthew. Jesus submits himself to his fate voluntarily. He is the obedient, the just one, the perfect fulfiller of the Law, but as he knows the Law, not as the Pharisees and the scribes who are expert in it. His conduct is such as to fulfill "all of God's demands," justice above all (3:15). This will be true in his Passion no less than at his baptism. Fulfillment, for Matthew, means that God's will is done perfectly through some event more comprehensive than the initial foreshadowing.

JESUS' CONDUCT in TRIAL and PASSION CONSISTENT with HIS TEACHINGS

In the mocking scene in which Jesus is hanging on the cross, for example, the challenge thrown to him to come down is, "if you are God's Son" (27:40). But this is a Matthean addition to Mark. Similarly, Jesus is taunted for his reliance on God and told to call on him for rescue. "After all, he claimed, 'I am God's Son'" (27:43*b*). This likewise is not found in Mark. These Passion-narrative texts have been anticipated by the devil's challenge, "If you are the Son of God . . ." (4:3), and Mary's conceiving "by the Holy Spirit" (1:20) of an offspring who is thought of as Emmanuel, "God is with us" (1:23).

Jesus is to be handed over to be crucified, with the implication by the author that such is God's will (26:2). He cannot ask his Father to set him free lest the Scriptures go unfulfilled ("it must happen this way"; 26:54). He submits freely because he wishes to lay hold of the inaugural end-time event—his death and resurrection—with both hands.

There are echoes in the Passion story of the innocence and justice Jesus teaches in the Sermon on the Mount, including his initial silence and subsequent refusal to answer under oath when the high priest orders him to do so (26:63-64; cf. 5:33-37), although he does respond in some fashion. In the garden he prays to his Father (26:39, 42), as he had taught others to pray (6:10*b*), "Thy will be done." Matthew alone has Judas call Jesus "innocent" (27:24), and Pilate call him "just" (27:24, in some manuscripts). Again, he is, for Pilate's wife, "that just man" (27:19), an uncharacteristic description by a Roman woman but understandable when one considers that what Matthew intends is a perfectly Law-observing Jew, a *tsaddik*, or just one. The word is missing in certain manuscripts, hence the reading, "that man," in which case she would be calling attention only to his innocence.

Everyone in Matthew's Passion story committed to the Law transgresses it somehow—Judas, Caiaphas, Peter. Jesus alone fulfills it throughout. The betrayer is made by Matthew to take the initiative in putting a price on his deed (26:15), in marked contrast to Jesus' advice: "The gift you have received, give as a gift" (10:8*b*). Gerhard Barth, who highlights many of the relations between the Passion narrative and earlier Matthean material, asks if Jesus' injunction, "Put back your sword where it belongs; those who use the sword are sooner or later destroyed by it" (26:52), may not be foreshadowed in 5:39, "Offer no resistance to injury (literally, to one who is evil)."[1] In any case, the saying is clearly inserted for a hortatory purpose. Jesus' statement, "Friend, do what you are here for" (v. 50), is so couched as to present Jesus' betrayal by Judas as a fulfillment of Scripture (cf. vv. 54, 56).

Looking specifically at Matthew's modifications of Mark, whom he follows closely except for the material special to him, our first observation is that he eliminates the "scribes" as out of place in the story of Jesus' arrest (26:47; contrast Mark 14:43). He also supplies the correct name of the high priest, Caiaphas (26:57), missing in Mark. Mark and Luke nowhere include it; John does so obliquely, through the Annas–Caiaphas relation (18:13), together with the phrase that Caiaphas was "high priest that year" in the sense of "that fateful year." Matthew implies, along with Mark, that the scribes and the elders were convened (the word *synedrion* literally means "assembly hall"), in the residence (or courtyard) of the high priest by saying that Peter approached it (26:57ff.). Matthew changes Mark's verb for their act of assembling to bring it into line with the Septuagint version of Psalm 2:2, "The princes conspire together against the LORD and against his anointed." Matthew observes of Peter, somewhat ominously, that he went into the courtyard, not to "warm himself at the fire" (Mark 14:54) but to "see the end" (26:58; cf. the use of the word for "end" in 24:6, 14, to designate the end of the age), suggesting the eschatological significance of the death of Jesus. Such is Matthew's certainty that this death marks the consummation of an epoch.

A COMMONPLACE on the TEMPLE'S END-TIME DESTRUCTION MADE a CHARGE against JESUS

The Matthean account of the search for testimony against Jesus by "the chief priests, with the whole Sanhedrin" (26:59) impugns their motives even more than Mark's does by calling the testimony they were after "false testimony" (ibid.). He also shortens Mark, who denies that there was any agreement among the witnesses, by having two of them come forward to say the same thing (vv. 60-61). The tradition that Jesus had prophesied the destruction of the temple evidently came from an earlier period in his public life (Mark 13:2 = Matt. 24:2 = Luke 21:6) and was introduced into the trial narrative as one of the chief charges of the priests against him. Matthew removes Mark's adjectival phrase about temples "made by human hands" and "not made by human hands" (14:58), no doubt finding it a "spiritualized" version, less probable historically. This change accords with Matthew's interest in continuity, for he refers to "the Temple *of God*" and says "I will rebuild it," whereas Mark speaks disparagingly of "*this* Temple" and says "I will build another." Matthew also changes "I will destroy" (Mark 14:58) to "I can destroy" (Matt. 26:61), but this is only a translation variant bringing the Greek closer to a supposed Aramaic original.

The hope of a new and more glorious Temple in the messianic age seems to have been widespread; hence it is not clear why Jesus' enunciation of a commonplace should have been received with consternation.[2] The Gospel tradition is that Jesus not only said what was commonly said in apocalyptic discourse (Mark 13:2 and parallels), but that he said he would do the destroying, a claim that figured in his condemnation (Mark 14:58 and variants, including John 2:19-20).

How could the first saying become the basis of a second one which ascribed a different meaning to Jesus? (Compare Matthew 23:38; 24:3; then compare the altered sense of the saying, implicating Jesus, in 26:61 and 27:40.) The prophecies ascribed to Jesus in 23:34-36 (par. Luke 11:49-51) and 37-39 (par. Luke 13:34-35) were originally Jewish oracles, with Wisdom as the speaker.[3] The general statement attributed to him by Matthew that one stone would not remain standing on another (24:2) was simply a repetition of an oracle of the LORD at the completion of Solomon's temple that, should Israel not remain faithful, it would "become . . . a byword among all the nations, and this Temple become a heap of ruins" (1 Kings 9:7-8).

Bultmann resorts to his eschatological myth of the Primeval Man for an explanation of the various apocalyptic predictions, including Matthew 26:61, holding that the myth could have resulted in this and similar sayings of Jesus (Mark 13:2; 14:58; 15:29; John 2:19; Acts 6:14). If, as he speculates, there was current in Jewish heretical circles a prophecy of cosmic catastrophe, it could have included the prediction of the destruction of the Temple.[4]

An easier explanation and one that should not be dismissed out of hand is that Jesus was responsible in his own person for some utterance or utterances that were construed as a threat to destroy the temple. The logion in John 2:19 ("Destroy this temple and in three days I will raise it up") and the Evangelist's interpretation that follows are probably based on something Jesus said, commented on in light of his resurrection.

Whatever the historical substrate, Matthew wishes to imply that two witnesses agreed (26:60) on what had been a true prophecy of Jesus, namely, that he would destroy the temple of God and rebuild it in three days. By the time the logion has reached the trial narrative it has acquired for those who believe in Jesus the Johannine meaning of "the temple of his body," even if, as spoken, it had referred to the actual edifice.

We need not go beyond Jeremiah to find a paradigm for Jesus' prophecy about destruction in Jerusalem: "The priests and prophets said to the princes and to all the people, 'This man deserves death; he has prophesied against this city, as you have heard with your own ears'" (Jer. 26:11). When it was pointed out on this occasion that Micah of Moreseth used to prophesy in the days of King Hezekiah that Jerusalem should become "a heap of ruins, and the temple mount a forest ridge" (26:18), there was no threat of death in response, only a reaction of fear of the LORD. Matthew depicts the chief priests, the scribes and elders, and the whole Sanhedrin (26:57, 59) of Jesus' day as resembling the priests and prophets of Jeremiah's time ("You must be put to death!" Jer. 26:8) more than the contemporaries of Micah in the days of Hezekiah.

Matthew has the high priest attempt to put Jesus under oath (*exorkizō*) before the living God to tell whether he is "the Christ, the son of God" (26:63). The adjuration is not historically probable in its wording (the formula is Christian), but it adds to the solemnity of the occasion and leads to Jesus' practical refusal to be bound by oath. His reply, "It is you who say it" (v. 64), is probably not an evasion; certainly it is not the formulation of an oath. Hence it is neither denial nor affirmation of Jesus' status as Messiah (with which "Son of God" is taken by the Evangelist to be equivalent). It is Matthew who has changed the response away from the "I am" of Mark 14:62. Hence, in neither Gospel is the response to be confused with a declaration of messiahship by the historical Jesus. Most probably Jesus is being made, by the phrase "It is you who say it," to have nothing to do with an oath, and to declare at the same time what the church already knows: that he is Messiah and Son of God.[5]

The *plēn* that follows immediately (Matt. 26:64) is adversative, "but," and is meant to contrast the church's faith in the Jesus of the present with the one who will be revealed in eschatological glory: "But, I say to you, henceforth you will see the Son of man sitting at the right hand of the Power and coming on the clouds of heaven." Matthew brings Mark (whose reading in 14:62 corresponds to the Masoretic Text and Theodotion) into line with the LXX of Daniel 7 by substituting "on" for "with" clouds. He inserts a time phrase (v. 64) which can mean "henceforward" or "soon." Whichever it means here, the language of apocalyptic with its reference to Psalm 110:1 is not to be held to chronological categories. Certainty of the fact of a future happening is enough. Matthew (26:66) follows Mark (14:64) in having the high priest ask his colleagues their opinion and in finding Jesus deserving of death because of the blasphemy they have supposedly just heard. He does, however, eliminate a word of Mark that may be proper to judicial sentence, they "condemned" or "judged" him, satisfying himself with the neutral "they answered."[6] Matthew omits the detail of blindfolding from Mark as if it were self-evident (v. 67). *Christe,* O Anointed One (v. 68), is a taunt delivered to a false Messiah.

MATTHEW'S FURTHER MODIFICATIONS of MARK and SPECIAL INSERTIONS

The alterations in Matthew's account of Peter's denial are relatively few and inconsequential. As was pointed out in the last chapter, note 6, Weeden, following Schreiber and Tyson, believes that Mark in his portrayal of the disciples is engaged in a polemic against them. Thus, Peter's rejection of Jesus (Mark 14:66-71) is taken to be part of a larger pattern stressing their negativism and obstinacy.[7] If this view is correct, Matthew does not scruple to follow Mark in his low estimate of the apostolic company. He omits the detail of Peter's warming himself (Mark 14:67) and has the serving girl call Jesus "the Galilean" rather than "the Nazorean" (Matt. 26:69, par. Mark 14:67), inserting "Jesus the Nazorean" later at verse 71. Matthew's Peter denies Jesus "in front of everyone" (v. 70) and "with an oath" (v. 72), getting more explicit in his second denial, "I do not know the man" (ibid.), than in Mark. The phrase "Even your accent gives you away" (v. 73) is a further Matthean explication. He likewise adds "bitterly" to the account of Peter's weeping, and tidies up Mark's prophecy of a threefold denial by the time of a second cockcrow (14:72) by having a cock crow once (Matt. 26:74). He then brings Jesus' prophecy into line with this change (v. 75).

Matthew's account of morning activity by the Sanhedrin ignores what has happened the night before just as thoroughly as does Mark's. The chief priests and elders decide (plot?) to put Jesus to death in the same phrase (27:1) as that used in 12:14 and 22:15. His fate is sealed before he goes off to Pilate.

The account of the death of Judas, 27:3-10, is clearly a Matthean insertion (cf. Mark 15:1 and 2). The story of Judas's interest in money (26:15) was probably pre-Matthean (cf. Mark 14:11), as was the notion that Scripture required his action (Mark 14:21; cf. Matt. 26:24); likewise, that his death was connected with a graveyard called Field of Blood (27:7; cf. Acts 1:15-20). The insertion is triggered by Judas's discovery that Jesus has been "condemned" (v. 3). This is Matthew's conclusion from whatever happened before the priests and elders. That it led to Jesus' being handed over to the governor in order to be put to death, Matthew has no doubt. He tells his story of Judas's regret and subsequent self-destruction as an elaborate introduction to the last of the many "formula quotations" in his Gospel, 27:9-10. This is a stitching together of Zechariah 11:12-13 and Jeremiah 32:6-15, with incidental reference to Jeremiah 18:2-3.[8] Stendahl takes Matthew's mention of Jeremiah, when it is the Zechariah quotation that is being fulfilled, to be "a slip or rather a confusion of memory."[9]

Basic to Matthew's fusing of the two texts at 27:9-10 is the similarity of the Hebrew words *yōtsēr* and *'otsār*, meaning, respectively, "potter" and "treasure/treasury."[10] The result of the priests' action is the unconscious fulfillment "on that occasion" (27:9) of prophecy, since the thirty pieces of silver that could not be put in the temple treasury (Zech. 11:13) were used to buy a field. Jeremiah had bought a field from his cousin Hanamel as a sign (Jer. 32:6-15), putting the sealed and the open deeds of purchase in a pottery jar (v. 14). He had also spoken of Israel under the figure of a vessel on a potter's wheel in God's hands (18:2-3). Matthew gives what he thinks is the hidden meaning of the Zechariah text, verse 13 of which reads: "So I took the thirty pieces of silver and threw them into the treasury in the house of the LORD." He does it by way of an involved targumic procedure which results in a reading of Zechariah that is not to be found in any Greek, Aramaic, or Hebrew Old Testament text.[11]

The charge on which Jesus is brought before Pilate (27:11) is the only one actionable before a civil court, namely, that he is a messianic revolutionary ("Are you the king of the Jews/Judaea?"). His answer is a cryptic "You say so," much like the "You have said so" of 26:25 and 64. In verses 12-14 Jesus remains completely silent before the accusations of the chief priests and elders. In all of this, there is no substantial departure from Mark in substance and very little in wording.

The same is true of Matthew's account of Barabbas. He does not specify murder in an uprising but contents himself with calling him a "notorious prisoner" (v. 16). It is interesting to speculate why he should have softened the charge against Barabbas, since the latter's sentence for insurrection is presumably the same one under which Jesus will shortly fall. It is true that Matthew stresses the alternative between the two as Mark has not done (v. 17). If the Sinaitic Syriac and Caesarean (Greek) texts are to be followed—though this is a doubtful procedure—Matthew knew them both as named "Jesus." Jesus is "called (the) Messiah" in Matthew (27:17), whereas in the parallel place Mark (15:9) has Pilate designate him "the king of the Jews." The Jewish people would not have called him that if they had written the title but "king of Israel" (see Matt. 27:42). Pilate is as aware in this Gospel as in Mark's that the Jewish leaders have handed him over "out of envy" (v. 18).

The improbable account of the warning Pilate's wife delivers to her husband as a result of a dream (27:19c) accords with Matthew's reliance on dreams in his first two chapters. It also highlights Pilate's innocence, something which the four Gospels are committed to, in contrast to the guilt of the chief priests and the elders who wish Jesus "destroyed" (v. 20). The "whole people" whom Matthew has answer in response has to be the "crowd" present in his narrative, distinguished from the Temple and Sanhedrin leadership. The phrase "His blood be on us and on our children" is biblical and is not an acceptance of guilt for Jesus' death, rather a claim of innocence to match Pilate's. See the use made of it in Jeremiah 26:15 and 51:35 noted above (chap. 1) and the phrase attributed to Paul, "Your blood be upon your own heads. I am not to blame" (Acts 18:6). The expression, far from being a self-inflicted curse, is a strong statement of innocence. Its meaning is, "If we had anything to do with it, let our descendants share the guilt. But we do not." It appears in later, mishnaic form in the tal-mudic tractate *Sanhedrin 37a,* where in capital cases the witness uses the invocation as a proof of his innocence. If he is lying, he is willing to have the blood of the accused fall on himself and his offspring until the end of the world. The phrase is always a claim of innocence, never of guilt. The scholarly world could do a great service by proclaiming long and loud what this phrase Matthew took from the Bible actually means, though the erroneous under-standing of it that has caused the Jewish people so much pain and persecution cannot be undone.

Matthew then has Pilate wash his hands to declare his inno-cence in gesture and word (a Jewish, not a Roman custom; cf. Deut. 21:6-9; Ps. 26:6a, 73:13b). The "whole people," that is, all present, reply in authentic Jewish fashion that they too bear no responsibil-ity for Jesus' blood (27:25).

Pilate yielded when he saw that his offer of Barabbas was gain-ing him nothing, but bringing on a riot instead (v. 24). Matthew has him order Jesus flogged, then delivered up (v. 26) as in Mark. This word "handed over" is frequent in the Passion accounts (Mark 14:10; 15:1; Matt. 27:26; Luke 23:25) and is heavily freighted with religious symbolism in Romans 8:32, as in all subsequent Chris-tian liturgies.

The place of Jesus' appearance before Pilate has been indeter-minate in Matthew. He is now led "inside the praetorium" (v. 27) for a mocking at soldiers' hands. The royal scepter in the form of a reed (v. 29) is a peculiarly Matthean detail; so is his "scarlet military cloak" (v. 28), Mark having reported a (royal?) purple (15:20) cloak. The mocking game of the soldiers ends in Jesus' being led away by the soldiers to be crucified (v. 31).

MATTHEW'S PRIMARY CONCERNS THEOLOGICAL

In considering Matthew's Passion narrative above, we have attended chiefly to his modifications of Mark, his main source, in light of his theological concerns as we know them from the rest of his Gospel. We have mentioned some but not all of the Passion material that is proper to him. The verses and pericopes from this putative M source include the following: 26:50; 26:52*b*-54; 27:3-10; 27:19, 24-25, 62-66; and 28:11-15 (a Pilate cycle); 27:43; 27:51*b*-53. Williams remarks on the lack of homogeneity of the M material, which he lists in full, and cites Streeter's observation regarding M's "Judaistic" tendency as contrasted with Q.[12] Stendahl prefers to avoid going into the problem of Matthew's sources. He confines himself to Matthew's use of Mark and Q, leaving aside any special attention to M or N (a putative source posited by B. W. Bacon, made up of haggadic traditions among Aramaic-speaking Christians of northeastern Syria).[13] Matthew, he says, is especially interested to show Christian faith and life as a "new constituency of Israel, where the last have become the first: a messianic community which is the true heir to the OT and which, after the exaltation of Jesus, contains also Gentiles, the very 'last.'"[14]

In Matthew's Passion, a tendency to view the Jewish leaders unfavorably is undeniable. That, however, is not primarily what the Evangelist is about. He wishes to convey that the one whom he portrays as innocent and just dies. This is not, however, to be taken "in the sense of an error of justice or of an infamous judicial murder, not even to magnify the guilt of the Jews thereby, but as a profoundly necessary event in God's plan of salvation."[15] The one who dies is the Lord, the Son of God. His exaltation (in the form of resurrection) to be the eschatological ruler necessarily follows on his death. Such is the paradox Matthew wishes to underscore, that Jesus' very suffering and dying are the revelation of him as ruler.

The "lowly king" enters Jerusalem (21:5) in order to be revealed as LORD. "From this time on" (23:39; 26:64), namely, from the time of his humiliation, he will be so made manifest. He is the representative of Israel who "fulfills all justice" (3:15) and thus brings God's judgment to victory (12:20 = Isaiah 42:3). The enmity of the Jewish leadership became a major theme as a result of the chasm that developed between church and synagogue, but in the beginning it was not so. It was a detail, howsoever important, in the outworking of the divine drama which Matthew was inviting all to view.

One last possibility should be recorded. Lloyd Gaston is of the opinion that Matthew has taken over from Mark the idea that the parousia of Jesus and the transition to the Gentile mission occurred in 70 CE (the latter view associated with Lohmeyer, Lightfoot, and Marxsen). The fall of Jerusalem was for Mark both a sign of the last judgment and an outcome of the death of Jesus.[16] That hypothesis is as good as the arguments alleged in its support. What is less arguable is Matthew's attempt at a theology of history in chapter 24 and the latter part of 25. There he sets about explaining all the blood that had been shed in the catastrophe of 66–70 CE. He has condemned the Pharisees bitterly in chapter 23 as a cipher for his contemporary opponents of the Gospel as part of this explanation ("Truly I tell you, all this will come upon the present generation," 23:36). He is facing the burning question which all within Israel faced: How could God have allowed the destruction of the Temple and so many of God's people?

Matthew's setting down of the people's cry, "His blood be on us and on our children" at 27:25, far from being meant as an incitement to persecution, would then have been an attempted explanation of all the bloodshed that the people had witnessed in the four-year period of siege. In the prophetic tradition it was a judgment against those bearing authority in Israel, like many judgments that had gone before it. If such was the setting within which Matthew placed the biblical outcry, then "Very much against his own intention . . . [he] became one of the principal sources of the persecution of Israel, which has haunted the history of the church down to our own day."[17]

Chapter 5

The INQUEST and TRIAL NARRATIVES in the GOSPEL according to LUKE

W e continue our search to discover the theological and apologetic concerns of the various Evangelists in light of which they shaped the traditional materials they had. In the case of Mark, it is not easy to arrive at conclusions about the stage of development his materials had reached before he modified them. Matthew's reliance on Mark's Passion (51 percent of his words agree wholly or in part with those of Mark, the balance being mainly popular stories) simplifies the question somewhat. With Luke there is enough that is peculiar to him that the question surrounding the Third Gospel is almost certain to take the form of the meaning of these special traditions. Perhaps the best way to introduce the theory of a special Lukan Passion source, which will be central to our treatment in this chapter, is to indicate which are the evident departures in Luke's Gospel from the main Mark–Matthew stream. We adopt the theory, however, that he edited a special source with the aid of Mark, rather than that he revised Mark in the light of his source. Our technique makes difficult any clear distinction between Luke's theology and that of his source.

Beginning at chapter 22, which opens with the chief priests plotting in fear of the people, Luke's first two verses are like Mark 14:1-2, even if severely edited down. He then omits the anointing of Jesus at Bethany (Mark 14:3-9) and goes immediately to the betrayal by Judas. This he attributes, unlike Mark and Matthew, to Satan (22:3). John will do the same (13:2, 27). Luke follows Mark in saying that the agreed-upon price is in "money" (silver, 22:5), not Matthew's "thirty pieces" taken from Zechariah. He also has army officers in on the plotting, not chief priests only (v. 4).

The LUKAN SUPPER and GETHSEMANE NARRATIVES; PETER'S DENIALS

Luke makes "the *first* day of Unleavened Bread" (Mark–Matthew) simply "the day of Unleavened Bread" (v. 7), probably to simplify Jewish custom, and designates the unnamed disciples who see to the preparations as Peter and John (v. 8). For the rest, he follows Mark in this narrative as Matthew has done. He begins to depart from his Markan model when Jesus eats with the "apostles" (v. 14), not "the twelve" (Mark 14:17) or "the twelve disciples" (Matt. 26:20), and with mention of "when the hour arrived," not "as it grew dark." Verses 15-18 are unique to Luke, suggesting a source: Jesus tells his friends how greatly he has desired to eat this Passover; then he utters a twofold vow. First, he will not eat it again until it is fulfilled in the reign of God (v. 16); second, he will not drink of the fruit of the vine until the reign of God has come (v. 18).

Some authors, like Vincent Taylor, think that, on both linguistic (i.e., word use and word count) and structural grounds, there is good reason to trace verses 14-18 to a non-Markan source. The passage resembles 1 Corinthians 11:26 in the form its eschatological concern takes ("until the coming of the reign of God"; cf. Paul's "until he come"), and in general conveys the primary meaning of the Last Supper for Luke, namely, that the cup and the bread are signs to be fulfilled when the reign or rule arrives.[1] The problems of Luke 22:19*b*-20 are special to this Gospel.[2] Verses 21-23 (cf. Mark 14:18-21; Matt. 26:21-25), which contain Jesus' prediction of his betrayal, are probably a non-Markan narrative except for verse 22, which seems to be a Markan insertion (72 percent of its words are common to Luke and Mark).[3]

The narrative of verses 24-27, the dispute over who among the disciples should be regarded as the greatest, does not give sufficient evidence of depending on Mark, hence is to be assigned to the special Lukan material. Similarly, the saying about continuing with Jesus in his trials and sitting on thrones judging the twelve tribes (vv. 28-30) comes from a source other than that of Matthew 19:28, close though that is in content. Luke's verse 29, "I for my part assign to you the dominion my Father has assigned to me," is without parallel. The eating and drinking with Jesus at table in the messianic reign, however, is a theme to be found in Luke 14:15; 22:15 and 18.

The sifting of Simon like wheat, Luke 22:31-33, resembles the prologues of Job and Zechariah 3:1-3, but it is palpably non-Markan. Verse 34, the prophecy of Peter's triple denial before cockcrow, is a "later Markan addition to the narrative."[4]

Verses 35-38 are "wholly peculiar to Luke," being intended as a reference back to 10:4 when everything was different with the disciples as regards preparedness for their mission.[5] Linguistic analysis establishes the distinctively Lukan character of this passage of four verses (the incidence, for example, of "likewise," "For I tell you," "and indeed," "Lord"). Luke seems to have edited his source here only lightly, a conclusion proper to everything from 14 to 38 except the Markan verses at Luke 22:22 and 34 and those at 19*b*-20 from the liturgical source. The suggestion that at one time verse 28 followed immediately on 20 (assuming the latter's genuineness) seems to have merit. The disciples, in offering two swords (v. 38), understand in a literal way Jesus' sense of the hostility toward him that will bring on his end. "Sword" in verse 36, where Jesus said, "Let him who has none . . . buy one," is meant metaphorically (cf. Matt. 10:34), but the metaphor about a future time of privation and opposition is entirely serious. It is not to be countenanced that Jesus had any such violence as that of the disciples in mind, as his impatient termination of the exchange indicates and, later, of the swordplay on the Mount of Olives (22:50).[6]

The agony in the garden (22:39-46) seems non-Markan in origin, with the exception of 46b ("Get up, and pray that you may not be subjected to the trial"). All but the initial verb here is from Mark 14:38. The details of the strengthening angel and the sweat as of blood (vv. 43-44) are not found in the oldest manuscripts, although their canonicity is not questioned. Where there are elements in common with the first two Gospels (e.g., Jesus' departure from his disciples "a stone's throw" away to pray and his prayer to his Father, vv. 41-42) the wording is not Markan in style. Some have held 39-46 to be a free Lukan composition joining the Last Supper to the arrest, but it seems much better explained as Luke's edited version of a narrative he already possesses in written or oral form.

Verses 52b-53a ("Have you come out with swords and clubs as if I were a bandit? When I was with you day after day in the temple, you did not lay hands on me") give every indication of being a Markan insertion (from 14:48-49) into a non-Markan source, Luke 22:47-54a, about the arrest of Jesus. Nonetheless, the high incidence of words in common with Mark suggests that Luke did his editing with Mark before him, especially 47a in light of Mark 14:43. The emphasis on the kiss by Judas as a sign seems different in Luke from Mark. Moreover, the healing of the servant's severed *right* ear (22:51b) is so out of character with other Gospel healings that it would best be explained by a special source or a historical reminiscence, not outlawing Luke's graphic prose.

The high occurrence of Markan words and phrases in Luke's denial of Jesus by Peter (22:54b-61) suggests reliance on Mark chiefly (14:54, 66-72). In both Gospels the incident takes place on the evening of the arrest. Since Luke has one hearing only before elders, chief priests, and scribes, and that at daybreak (v. 66), his denial scene precedes both mocking (22:63-65)—presumably also at night—and hearing (22:66-71). In Mark it follows the two incidents. Luke uses some of his favorite words in this narrative, thereby betraying his heavy editorial activity. The details of the lighting of a fire (v. 55) and the interval of an hour after which another person (a man, like the second challenger, also male, not a servant girl; differently in the parallels) identified Peter as Galilean (v. 59) are not found elsewhere. Luke's earlier reference to the denial (22:34) had been Markan, so this later dependence does not surprise us. Mark may be his only written source for the denial. It does not seem necessary to require any special written material or an oral source common to Luke and John to account for the above details—or the possible reminiscence of Jesus' having "turned around and looked at Peter" (v. 61a). Luke's own editorial activity would suffice.

The Evangelist's wording in the mocking scene (22:63-65) is so unlike Mark's (14:65) with its dependence on Isaiah 50:6 that he seems to have composed his account by rewriting material from his special source, inserting some of his favored vocabulary.

JESUS before the SANHEDRIN, PILATE, and HEROD ANTIPAS

The above examination of the various brief narratives in Luke 22 should bring us to what is our central concern, namely, the summoning of Jesus by elders, chief priests, and scribes before "their Council" (v. 66). This hearing before Jewish authority is covered in verses 66-71. It is hard to say what Luke's editorial activity is here. He seems to possess a tradition about a morning trial in which everything hinges on the question of Jesus' messiahship. The charge of blasphemy does not appear, nor is there mention of the testimony of false witnesses. The Temple saying of Mark 14:58 does not occur in Luke. Jesus' reply (to "them," v. 67, not to the high priest) uses Psalm 110:1 ("From now on, there will be the Son of Man, *sitting at the right hand of* the Power [of] God"), but in a quite different way from Mark (who had "You will see the Son of Man sitting . . ."), even though verse 69 probably depends on Mark 14:62. The use of Markan words runs about 35 percent in these six verses (33 out of 94 words), something that is almost unavoidable in light of the subject matter. Only at verse 71, "What further need have we of testimony? We ourselves have heard it from his own mouth," does Luke closely resemble Mark (14:63*b*), who speaks of "witnesses" rather than "testimony," and of blasphemy, as Luke does not. All things considered, Luke's differences from Mark on the time of this inquiry and the order in which it appears in his narrative are such that he must have used another source. Nonetheless, the possibility of his use of Markan "reminiscences" is not to be ruled out.[7]

Jesus is led from the Sanhedrin to Pilate by "the entire assembly" (23:1). Recall that in 18:32 Luke has Jesus prophesy his deliverance up to the Gentiles (only). The first five verses of chapter 23 tell of the examination of Jesus by Pilate in words that are marked by Lukan characteristics except for verse 3. In that verse ("Pilate asked him, 'Are you the king of Judaea/the Jews?' He answered, 'That is your term'"), sixteen words occur that are common to Luke and Mark. If Luke's source did not contain this verse, he would need it to link up verses 2 and 4. Pilate's "I do not find a case against this man" (v. 4) does not make sense without some such bridge. Jesus has been charged with subverting the nation and not paying taxes to Caesar (v. 2). Pilate will be acting reasonably in finding Jesus innocent only if he can declare him free of a charge which, as a civil official, he does not find actionable (see 23:14). Luke apparently discovers the escape he needs in Mark 15:2 and inserts it as his verse 3.

If 23:1-5 is a Lukan source reworked except for verse 3, verses 6-16—the examination before Herod Antipas—are peculiarly Luke's composition. So many of his characteristic words appear in this pericope (an exception is Mark's word for "scribes," v. 1; Luke normally prefers "lawyers"; but see 23:10) that there is little about it to suggest a source. The case is strengthened by the fact of Luke's writing in Acts 4:27 (after he has quoted Ps. 2:1-2), "They gathered in this very city, . . . Herod and Pontius Pilate in league with the Gentiles and the peoples of Israel," in which description

Herod would represent the "kings of the earth" in the psalm, Pilate the "princes," the Roman soldiers the "Gentiles," and the tribes of Israel the "peoples."

In framing the narrative in his Gospel, Luke shows some knowledge of Johannine tradition. John has Pilate declare Jesus innocent three times (18:38*b*; 19:4-6); the same is found in Luke 23:4, 15, 22. With the resumption of examination by Pilate (vv. 18-25; v. 17 is textually doubtful), Luke can be modifying Mark (compare 23:19 with Mark 15:7; 23:22 with Mark 15:14) or his special source. Probability favors the latter, especially because similarities between verses 23-24 and Mark are so few. Verse 25, which highlights the enormity of the people's choice of Barabbas over Jesus, a carefully constructed summary by Luke appended to finish off the section, may be a version of Mark 15:15 (note the verbs for "released" and "delivered over" in both).

LUKE'S HYPOTHETICAL PASSION SOURCE DISTINGUISHED from MARK

This inquiry into possible sources of the Lukan trial narratives is largely dependent on the painstaking work of Vincent Taylor.[8] He, in turn, has banked heavily on the researches of Schürmann,[9] Rehkopf,[10] and Easton.[11] The reason for the work of source analysis should be self-evident. Knowing something of Mark's theological outlook, and Matthew's in adapting Mark to the needs of his readers, we should acquaint ourselves with what seems to be another source than the Markan one on the events of the trial. Not only will be compiler of this source have had his traditions with which to work and his presuppositions; so, too, will Luke. By the inclusions and omissions of each writer, and by Luke's recourse to Mark in particular (away from the source he largely follows), we should learn something about not one but two additional early Christian mentalities. What can we discover first about Luke's source and then about Luke himself?

The Lukan Passion source emphasized the end-time hope aspect of the Last Supper (22:14-18). To it were added verses (19*b*-20) taken from another liturgy (Antioch, as against Caesarea?) which centered on the saving activity of Jesus.

Luke's source has Jesus speak of a desire to eat the Passover meal before he suffers (22:15), which would agree with the tradition in John that the appearance before Pilate took place on Preparation Day (18:28; 19:14). The two together support the view that the final meal is not a Passover meal, in contrast to the view that the Last Supper was such, an idea that we get from Mark only, since Matthew merely follows him.

The source contents itself with attributing Judas's action to Satan's influence (22:3). This could identify the traditions of Judas's kiss (Mark 14:44-45) and of greed as his motivation (Matt. 26:15; John 12:6) as later elaborations, in the second case a deduction from the fact of betrayal.

The source puts the blow with the sword in the garden before the attempted arrest (22:50; so does John 18:10), as if it were a defensive measure. Mark places it after (14:47), making it more an active attempt to free the prisoner. Brandon predictably assumes that the more primitive Mark has unwittingly betrayed a violent spirit in Jesus and his company which the later Luke softens for apologetic reasons.[12] In the theory of the source's primitive character, Jesus disapproves the disciple's act. He does the same in John (18:11), who makes it the occasion for a logion of Jesus about drinking the cup the Father has given him. This puts Jesus' pacific response to the violence in an earlier position and the aggressiveness of the bystander (Mark 14:46) in a later.

The source attributes the mocking to the men guarding Jesus (22:63-65). This is entirely more likely than that the priests should have done it, as in Mark (14:65).

In the source, Jesus parries the Sanhedrin's question about his messiahship (22:67), much as John has him do in other circumstances (10:24-25). The ambiguity is such ("If I tell you, you will not believe me, and if I question you, you will not answer"; cf. 20:8) that the response cannot be a later formulation as Mark 14:62 clearly is. John 10:24-25 seems to have drawn on the same tradition as Luke in 22:67, 70.

The political charges against Jesus in the source (23:2, 5), which consist of stirring up the people to the point of tax resistance, ring true historically as counts on which he would be vulnerable before the empire. Luke probably employed the Markan insertion (Luke 23:3; almost certainly from Mark 15:2) to render Pilate's response that he found "no case against this man" more credible. The threefold charge would, of itself, scarcely bring on such a response. Mention of kingship could be taken as nonpolitical if it were interpreted religiously as "the king of the Jews/ Judaea," something that the Markan insertion tries to accomplish. Even so, the gap is not closed.

The most probable background for the reconciliation of Pilate and Herod over the matter of Jesus (23:12) is Psalm 2:2, in which princes conspire "against the LORD and against his anointed." This is coupled with Isaiah 53:7 ("he opened not his mouth") to account for Jesus' failure to answer (v. 9). The story as written by Luke— whether from his source or not is hard to say—can be related historically to Pilate's slaughter of Herod's Galilean subjects (13:1-2) and to Luke's earlier statement that, after the beheading of John, Herod was very curious to see Jesus (9:9) and even wished to kill him (13:31).

The resumed inquiry of Pilate in the source (23:18-25) contains historical fragments of the Barabbas offer, Pilate's unwillingness to condemn Jesus (supported by John), and his ultimate responsibility for the sentencing.

The source's crucifixion narrative (23:27-48) is an artful and cohesive account even without its Markan touches (vv. 34*b*, 38, 44-45, 49). Perhaps the best proof of its independence from Mark is the simple declaration of the centurion that Jesus was a just man (v. 47), whereas Mark makes him utter a faith statement, "Surely this man was the son of God" (15:39; *REB,* "must have been a son of God"). Luke follows, and develops, an independent source in his resurrection narrative, probably influenced by his knowledge of Mark. Jesus' appearance to the eleven (24:36-49) shows a clear apologetic concern, with its emphasis on the reality of the resurrection (vv. 39-42). Even more important is the inability of two disciples who knew him well, Cleopas and another, to recognize him, as was the case of the Magdalene (John 20:15). The two incidents are means of indicating that in his altered state as risen he was not resuscitated and returned to the old life. Luke has him recognized for who he is in the church's meal of broken bread (24:35), John similarly in the sharing of bread with fish added (21:13).

If we look back on the narratives of the arrest and the appearances of Jesus before the Sanhedrin and Pilate as they occur in Luke's source, they yield the following data:

- The soldiers of the Temple guard come out to apprehend him (22:52a; "chief priests" occurs too, a bare possibility but probably metonymy for those sent by them, as in Mark 14:43b).

- Jesus opposes violent resistance to his captors (vv. 49-51).

- Jesus is brought to "the house of the high priest" (v. 54) and there mocked by the men guarding him (vv. 63-65); at daybreak he is brought by "the elders, the chief priests, and the scribes" before "their council," who ask him if he is the Messiah and, in a separate question, the Son of God. He is evasive as to the first title and acknowledges the second. Having had Jesus sidestep the Sanhedrin's question in a way uncharacteristic of Luke, the source then joins Daniel 7:13 and Psalm 110:1 in truncated fashion and employs the Semitism "the Power" for "God" by making Jesus say, "From now on, the Son of man will have his seat at the right hand of the Power of God" (22: 69). This may be Luke's modification of Mark 14:52, but his citation of Daniel 7:13 in 21:27 shows that he knows how to use the phrase correctly. *It is much more likely that the version in Luke's Gospel comes from his source.* (The Lukan phrase that speaks of acknowledging the Son of Man "before the angels of God," 12:8, does not seem close enough to cite in this connection.) Moreover, the usage in Luke speaks of simple enthronement and not of coming with clouds, as if the verse were employed here solely to raise the question about the second title, "the Son of God."

- The charges of agitation against the Romans by Jesus, even his claiming royal status, are not taken seriously by Pilate; he says he has examined him and has "no charge against him arising from your allegation" (23:4, cf. vv. 15, 22).

• The chief priests and scribes stand by accusing Jesus vehemently at Herod's court to which Pilate has sent him (23:10).

• Pilate persists in his (threefold) declaration that he has found nothing in Jesus that calls for death; he says he will order him flogged (v. 22) and release him.

• Pilate, yielding to the violent shouts of the crowd, "gave his verdict that their demand should be granted" (v. 24); he then "handed Jesus over as they wished" (v. 25).

THEOLOGY and HISTORICAL TRADITION BLENDED in LUKE'S PASSION SOURCE

The primitive character of the Christology and soteriology of the source is readily contrasted with those of Luke's Gospel and Acts. Luke elsewhere favors a son-servant Christology; his Passion source, more primitive, does not contain it. Luke largely leaves the source untouched, with its preferences for the reign of Christ and its silence as to the servant and sonship themes.

Luke himself looks upon the work of Christ as primarily one of obedience to his Father's will. Sacrifice or vicarious atonement do not interest him (hence the omission of Mark's giving his life "as a ransom for the many," 10:45). The theme of Jesus' sacrifice in place of others occurs in his special liturgical source (22:19-20; not his special Passion source). Luke omits Jesus' anguished outcry of forsakenness (Mark 15:34) and has him commend his spirit to his Father (23:46).

In brief, then, the primitive Passion source of Luke shows us a blend of theology and historical tradition that could date to the Antioch of the forties. Its primitive character is of great importance, testifying as it does to the existence of certain historical traditions which are in no way dependent on Mark. Chief of these is that of an interrogation before some priestly body at an early morning hour (not at night as in the Mark–Matthew tradition) which has as its finding Jesus' guilt. He is subverting (23:2) the Jewish people, that is, leading them astray (23:14) from doing what they ought as Roman subjects. The phrase may have the stronger meaning of inciting to revolt but the verb *apostréphō* has a history in Hellenized Jewish usage of meaning deceiving Jews over the oneness of God. As a result, "the entire assembly led him before Pilate" (23:1).

LUKE'S CHRISTOLOGY REQUIRES THAT JESUS BE FOUND GUILTY and PILATE INNOCENT

Turning in detail to the Lukan version of Jesus' examination before the Sanhedrin (22:66-71), we discover that, just as in Mark's account, it is meant to be a climactic christological statement. Yet it seems sufficiently unlike what Luke holds elsewhere about the identity of the titles Messiah and Son of God (cf. 4:41; Acts 9:20, 21) that we must conclude that he finds it in his source and leaves it unchanged. The source omits the testimony about Jesus' promise to destroy the temple (Mark 14:57-61*a*; Matt. 26:60*b*-63*a*) and concentrates on the two titles "Messiah" (v. 67*a*) and "Son of God" (v. 70). Luke, in letting it stand, probably intends the first to express a political claim and the second a religious, namely, Jesus' divine sonship.[13]

The source does not let Jesus answer the first question. It has him correct "Messiah" to "Son of man" (v. 69) so as to dissociate him from the Jewish political concept, even though as a religious title Luke accords it to him readily (cf. 4:41; Acts 9:20, 22). The evasive answer of Jesus that Luke retains (v. 67*b*) may be the source's way of exposing the insincerity of the question; Luke himself has no doubt that Jesus is the Messiah. If it had been put in good faith the questioners would already know the answer. The response of Jesus in verses 67*b*-68 is complete in itself but leads to 69, in antithesis to the question as put. Hoping to avoid political misinterpretation, it sets the scene for the next, divine title. Primarily, Luke's source retains only the title Son of man from Daniel 7 and combines it with the quotation from Psalm 110:1. "He thereby produces for the first and only time a Son of man saying in which the main content is the *sessio ad dextram dei*."[14]

Matthew at this point (26:64) has Jesus say: "Soon you will see the Son of Man." In Luke it is changed to, "From now on the Son of Man will have his seat. . . ." Continuing, Luke here omits all reference to Daniel 7:13, even though he knows the text (17:24; 21:27). This raises the question of whether Luke is simply transmitting a primitive tradition which he prefers not to alter or is presenting it in such a way that it accords perfectly with his overall theology. The latter view thinks he has taken the title from Daniel 7:13 but does not wish to feature an exaltation-parousia that men will look upon, least of all Jesus' questioners. That is, for Luke, not a soon-to-be-expected stage of events and surely not the next one, as it had been for Mark and Matthew. The view that we do not have Luke's theology in 22:66-70 but that of his source identifies those verses as depicting a scheme in which Messiah and Son of God are not yet equated, in circles where "divine Sonship is a repugnant concept sealing the doom of the claimant."[15]

In the opinion of Tödt, Luke is no less convinced than Mark or Matthew that the attitude of the high priest or priests constitutes a break with the past. The new era for Luke, however—with 22:69 as the turning point—is not the end time but the period of the church in which Christ will reign in heaven. Israel's redemptive history is over for Luke. The moment of Jesus' abasement is, at the same time, the turning point that marks the beginning of his sovereign rule. "From now on" there is "the glory of God, and Jesus standing at God's right hand" (Acts 7:55). "The parousia appears to have withdrawn into remoteness."[16] With the vow of Jesus not to drink the fruit of the vine until God's reign comes (22:18), the new age has begun. One period is over, another is inaugurated.[17]

These are the last times for Luke as for the other Synoptic Evangelists but experienced in a different way. The great matter for all three is Jesus' final victory, which the first two conceived of in terms of his imminent return. Luke is content to live on in the church in the certainty of Jesus' heavenly triumph. The reign the Son of Man exercises from there is invisible, hence the need to eliminate in the saying at 22:69 (par. Mark 14:62) the verb "you will see." The longing to "see one of the days of the Son of Man"

(17:22), although thwarted, is partly subsumed under the fulfill-ment of Jesus' enthronement (22:69). But the present situation is far from perfect (22:18). It is a long season of waiting until the full coming of the reign of God.

Jesus as Son of Man is the Exalted One. "'So you are the Son of God?' they asked in chorus" (v. 70a). In his reply to this, Jesus acknowledges his divine sonship, if in oblique phrasing. "All" (v. 70) have put the question, Flender thinks, including the reader of the Gospel.[18] The faith reality has been proclaimed to all. It is not possible to determine whether the "all" is Lukan or pre-Lukan. He often uses it in his editorial efforts, and such may be the case here. The response of the Sanhedrin, at least verse 71a, seemingly derived from Mark, helps Luke reach the end of his story quickly. Like the other Evangelists, he has the problem of reporting a Jesus who is rejected but who at the same time can be believed in. He does this by describing him as making a religious self-disclosure before Israel's highest body. That body grants that it has heard the claim from his own mouth (v. 71b) but rejects it as self-incriminating (v. 71a).

The question put by the Sanhedrin, stage one (22:67a), con-fines itself to popular opinion about Jesus in the ordinary terms of Davidic sonship. Stage two (v. 70) moves on to faith in him as the Son of God. Luke depicts the Sanhedrin as incapable of that faith, but this is not his main concern. As we know from the over-all thrust of his Gospel, he is throwing an existential challenge to his readers. If they have faith in Jesus as Son of God, they will make the reality of heaven present on the earth. Luke is concerned with a Spirit-filled community obedient to God's will. Unlike Mark's per-secuted awaiters of a vindicated Jesus who do not experience him as LORD, the church of Luke knows him present at "the right hand of the Power of God" giving them leadership as a community. He is not the Messiah only, for Luke, he is Messiah and Lord (2:11); hence the question must go unanswered in the terms on which it is posed.

Luke has carefully prepared for Jesus' appearance before Pilate. Jesus told his parable of the man who went off to a distant country to be crowned as king (19:11-27) "because he was near Jerusalem, where they thought that the reign of God was about to appear" (v. 11*b*). Jesus has equated true sonship of Abraham with salvation for this same Jericho audience (near Jerusalem? 19:9). He tells a tale of wise investment by two men but none by a third. The latter represents that large populace that will not have the nobleman be king over them.

The FINAL DAYS

Such is the immediate Lukan setting for Jesus' ascent to Jerusalem as a pilgrim. As the entourage comes from Bethphage and Bethany at the foot of the Mount of Olives to the city, the disciples chant the familiar song of welcome to festal pilgrims, Psalm 118. Luke amends its verse 26 ("Blessed be he who comes in the name of the LORD"), however, to read, "Blessed be he who comes *as the king* in the name of the LORD" (19:38). Immediately appended is a snatch of the angels' song from 2:14 but altered to read, "Peace in heaven and glory in the highest." The peace of heaven is the underlying condition of Jesus' kingship on earth for Luke. Jesus weeps over a city that does not know the path of peace (19:41-42), then makes his way directly to its Temple, the only scene of his activity. For his ejection of the traders there (vv. 45-46), the chief priests, scribes, and leaders of the people look for a way to destroy him (v. 47). It is against them that he tells his parable of the vineyard (20:9-17). It is they who send spies to trap him in his speech so that they may "hand him over to the office and authority of the governor" (v. 20). It is they whose duplicity he identifies, in the question they put about paying tribute to the emperor.

The setting is complete. The main charge against Jesus, his opposition to paying tribute to Caesar (23:2), has been shown in the chapters immediately preceding to be baseless. Pilate has no alternative but to find no case against him, whether the charge he examines be that of subversion, kingship, or nonpayment of tribute. Luke has taken the pains beforehand to show Jesus innocent of every charge but makes a further attempt by adding verse 3 from

Mark 15:2. He is undoubtedly engaging in a political apologetic here but, far more importantly, has laid the theological groundwork for establishing the heavenly character of Jesus' reign.

As has just been indicated, Luke is very probably informing the imperial authority of his own day that the accusations against the Christians are groundless. He makes the point that in the past the Roman governor had seen through the false charges of the Jewish leadership, even going so far as to declare Jesus innocent three times. The real criminals are insurgents and murderers (23:19, 25), not religious men whose claims lie outside the political order. Luke establishes Jesus' innocence before the three authorities of his day as he conceives them: the province, subject to the prefect; the puppet kingdom; and the city under priestly-elder rule. Jesus answers the priests theologically. He is silent before Herod, the powerless king. He answers Pilate, however cryptically.

Pilate, in Luke's Gospel, has been at such pains to find no cause against Jesus, despite hearing his oblique claim to messiahship, that he literally cannot condemn him. This absence of a verdict by Pilate is not accidental. Luke reads of one in Mark (15:15) but omits it here. He has Jesus delivered up, not "to be crucified" but "to their wishes" (23:25).

The climax of the trial for Luke is the evidence heard by Jesus' interrogators "from his own mouth" (22:71b). The same phrase has occurred before in 4:22; 11:54; 19:22, all of it special Lukan material.[19] Does Luke, or his source which he uses approvingly, think that Jesus appeared before an interrogatory hearing or a trial? No verdict is reported, yet the following terms contain hints of judicial action: "their council," the "assembly of the people" (both in v. 66), and "what further need have we of testimony?" (v. 71). Luke speaks of "their plan and their action" in 23:51 and "their rulers" having "condemned" him in Acts 13:27. His source, therefore, seems to be familiar with a tradition of adverse action against Jesus from which Luke does not dissociate himself.[20]

It is quite true that Mark's trial narrative, filled as it is with secondary material, was the initial description in our Gospels of Jesus' fate at the hands of religious leadership and imperial power.

Matthew elaborated on it, adding the outcry of innocence by "all the people" which has since caused so much mischief. Luke, to every appearance, worked from a pre-Markan source which contained a basically similar tradition. His description of the events is little improved by his occasional reliance on Mark, *but it cannot be held that the civil charges before Pilate of 23:3 are the sole historical reminiscence in his Gospel.* His is much more restrained in style than the first two Evangelists, omitting the dramatized elements found in Mark and Matthew. Nonetheless, his theology of synthesis found eminently suitable to his purpose a Jewish and Gentile collaboration in guilt, which signalized the end of an epoch. The new epoch was marked by Jewish and Gentile acceptance of the Holy Spirit under the lordship of Christ.

Chapter 6

The CAIAPHAS and PILATE
NARRATIVES in JOHN

M any authors over the past one hundred years have speculated on the existence of a source or sources underlying the Fourth Gospel. In 1910 Spitta, Bacon, and
Goguel all published book-length studies on the problem. The
research reached a high point in 1941 with the commentary of
Rudolf Bultmann.[1] This work proposed a "signs-source" (*Semeia-
Quelle*), a position in which many followed him, but also suggested
so many displacements and insertions into a theoretical original
that not many could commit themselves to the complex editorial
process he posited. D. Moody Smith did an analysis of Bultmann's
theory in 1965,[2] and Robert T. Fortna produced in 1970 a reconstruction of the hypothetical narrative source, a "*Gospel* of Signs"
rather than the signs-source Bultmann had called for.[3]

Fortna puts the signs of Jesus, after the Baptist's testimony
and the conversion of the disciples, in the following sequence:

the miracle at Cana (John 2); a nobleman's son healed (4:43-54); a miraculous draft of fish (chap. 21), and the multitude fed (chap. 6). The walking on water (chap. 6) provides an interlude which is not a sign. Then Lazarus is raised (chap. 11); Jesus meets a Samaritan woman (4:1-42); a man blind from birth is healed (chap. 9); and the victim of a thirty-eight-year illness is healed (chap. 5). This gives us seven signs in all, the first four above worked in Galilee, the last three in Judaea, with the conversation at Jacob's well in Samaria as another interlude.

Fortna's final sign is the death and resurrection of Jesus, which he concludes was dealt with in the source in this order: the cleansing of the temple (John 2:13-22) and the death plot (chap. 11), the anointing at Bethany and the triumphal entry (chap. 12), the arrest and Jesus in the high priest's house (chap. 18), the trial before Pilate (chaps. 18 and 19), the crucifixion and burial (chap. 19), and the resurrection (chap. 20).

THEORIES of a MARK-JOHN and a LUKE-JOHN RELATION

Ivor Buse has produced a short study which accepts the theory of Vincent Taylor that Mark was largely composed of non-Semitic narrative source A and a Semitic incidents source B.[4] In carrying out his researches, Buse found a high coincidence between the Johannine Passion narrative and the Markan material classified as B, and no significant likeness to the material classified as A. Specifically, the similarities noted by Buse are as follows:

		Mark	John
1.	The anointing of Jesus	14:3-9	12:3-8
2.	The betrayal	14:18 (14:17-21?)	13:21
3.	Jesus' prayer in Gethsemane	14:32-42	12:27-28, 31; 18:11

		Mark	John
4.	The assault on the high priest's servant	14:47	18:10-11
5.	Peter's denial	14:54; 66-67	18:18 (18:25-26)
6.	The trial before Pilate	15:2	18:33b-34
7.	The Barabbas story	15:9-10	18:39-40
8.	Handing over of Jesus to be crucified	15:15	19:16
9.	The mocking	15:16-18 Add 14:65	19:23, 5 Add 18:22

The material in the Markan column above is all assigned by Taylor to his source B, except for 14:17-21 (which he does mark as containing Semitisms although assigned to A) and 15:15.

Buse deduces that John has many striking resemblances, often word-for-word identity of expression (e.g., items 1, 6, 8 above) with Mark's B source. B is not a single source, actually, but all the elements inserted into A. This leads Buse to conclude that, as far as the Passion narrative goes, John must have been acquainted, not with Mark, but with one or more of his sources. Further, he is convinced that the independent existence of something like B before Mark incorporated it into his Gospel is established by the Johannine similarities he has discovered.

Peder Borgen goes further than Buse in his inquiry, concluding that units of Matthew and Luke, as well as of Mark, have been added to the Johannine tradition.[5] He scrutinizes the Passion-burial-resurrection narratives in their entirety. Especially relevant to our purpose is his examination of the considerable agreements of John with all the Synoptics, then with each individually in the story of Jesus' appearance before Pilate[6] and in the Annas–Caiaphas account.[7] Buse returns to the discussion with an inquiry into John's similarity to Matthew and Luke. He concludes that "the agreements between Matthew and John are neither numerous nor of a decisive character,"[8] and puts any coincidences down to similar streams of oral tradition, in default of weightier evidence.

The Lukan parallels to John in the Passion narrative are another matter: "the similarities are on such a scale as to make sheer coincidence a most improbable supposition."[9] The hypothesis of a common source or sources fits the facts better than one of any mutual knowledge. A number of the Lukan agreements with John occur in settings that were also in the B stratum of Mark's Passion narrative. Of these, the clearest are the similarities in the accounts of the trial of Jesus before Pilate; the announcement of the betrayal; and the identification of the ear severed by Simon Peter as the right ear. A justifiable deduction for Buse is that Luke as well as John knew the Passion-narrative parts that occur in Mark's B stratum. Where Luke and John concur in matters that go unmentioned by Mark, Mark's silence would be accounted for by his not using everything from a source that was secondary to him.

Centering on the trial material in John's source, we begin with the death plot. Fortna's researches build on the scholarship cited above that preceded him. We shall indicate when a particular matter occurs in his signs-source by designating it *SQ* (*Semeia-Quelle*). This is *not* Bultmann's signs-source but Fortna's signs-Gospel. *SQ* designates for him a "corrected and expanded version" of the presumed narrative source that John used.[10]

First in order in *SQ* comes the cleansing of the temple (2:14-16). To it the chief priests and Pharisees (John calls them the *Ioudaîoi* in vv. 18, 20 but Fortna does not think it part of the source; the usage of *SQ* is deduced from 18:3, which *is*) respond by asking what sign Jesus can point to whereby he does these things (2:18). He answers by saying, "Destroy this Temple, and in three days I will build it up" (v. 19). *SQ* consistently proves Jesus' messiahship by his works of power. It alone makes him the subject of the verb "to raise," here ("I will build it up") and in 12:1. Elsewhere in the New Testament it is God who does the raising.

There follow immediately in *SQ* verses 11:47*a*, the calling of a meeting of the Sanhedrin by "the chief priests and the Pharisees," and 11:53, the plan from that day onward to kill him.

The anointing of Jesus at Bethany comes next (12:1-8). Missing from *SQ* are the time reference, "six days before Passover" (v. 1) and John's editorial observation on Judas's motivation, verse 6. Then comes the triumphal entry into Jerusalem (12:12-15). *SQ*'s account of the Last Supper is probably scattered about in the following places: 12:27; 13:(1*b*), 2*a*, 4-5, 12-14, 18*b*, 21*b*, 26-27, 37-38; 14:31*b*; 16:32*b*.

Jesus is arrested (18:1-5*ab*), with the phrase in verse 4, "aware of all that would happen to him," omitted. *SQ* identifies, as those who came to the garden, a "cohort" and "guards" "of the chief priests and the Pharisees" (v. 3). They are mentioned again, as is a "tribune/officer," in the account of the severing of the right ear of the high priest's slave and the actual arrest of Jesus (vv. 10-12). These military men need not be Roman soldiers. Indeed, it is much more likely that they are not.[11]

Jesus is led to Annas first, the "father-in-law of Caiaphas who was the high priest that year" (18:13). Annas sends him to Caiaphas (v. 24). Simon Peter and a disciple known to the high priest come to the gate of the high priest's courtyard (vv. 15-16*a*). The high priest then questions Jesus (vv. 15-23), all as in John except that Jesus' answer in verse 20 consists only of, "I always taught in a synagogue or in the temple area." Another difference is that Peter's first denial, 16*b*-18, occurs after verse 23 (Jesus' spirited rejoinder following the sharp blow he receives from the guard) and before Peter's further denials (vv. 25-27). With verse 28*ab*, at daybreak Jesus is brought to the praetorium, which "they" did not enter lest they be defiled.

The trial before Pilate follows in this order: verses 33 (without the phrase "went back into the praetorium"), 37*a*, and 38*c*—a spare exchange in which Pilate asks if Jesus is the king of the Jews/ Judaea. He answers, "It is you who say it," and Pilate then says he finds no case against him. The shout of 19:15 to crucify Jesus interrupts. Verses 39-40 of chapter 18, on Barabbas, then take up the narrative. Next comes 19:6 in which chief priests and temple guard shout "Crucify him," to which Pilate on the judge's bench at Gabbatha responds by trying to release Jesus (12-14*a*). Scourging at

Pilate's command and mockery by the soldiers follows (19:1-2). Finally, "he handed him over to be crucified" (v. 16*a*).

The crucifixion, burial, and resurrection sequence of *SQ*, less germane to our purpose, is 19:16*b*-19, 20*b*, 23-24, 28-29, 30*b*, 25, 31-32, 34*a*, 36-38; 3:1; 19:39-42; 20:1-3, 5, 7, 9-12, 14, 16-20, 30-31.

SQ is probably of Syrian origin, according to Fortna. In any case, there is a knowledge of Palestinian tradition. Aramaic words go untranslated. Certain words like *Messias* and *Christos; rabbouni, kyrios,* and *didaskalos,* are used interchangeably. There is no deliberate use of the Jewish Scriptures; rather, a knowledge of them is taken for granted as in 4:5 (the land near Sychar which Jacob had given to Joseph). The purpose in the source is simple and clear, Fortna states on p. 225 in his "Origin and Purpose": to show to the potential Jewish convert that Jesus is the Messiah. *SQ* does not hesitate to use Jesus' miracles as "wonders." John will modify this element to "signs" that point to Jesus' mission. Practically all who are exposed to Jesus' power believe in him, like the royal official in 4:53. The relationship between Jesus' role as a "heavenly man" and his messiahship is not argued in *SQ*. This is remarkable in that there is little direct evidence that the Jewish Messiah was expected to be a wonder-worker. Perhaps the Moses-like quality of Jesus is the explanation. More likely still is his having been patterned after Elijah or Elisha. Fortna even hints at likenesses to Joseph ("Do whatever he tells you," 2:5; cf. Gen. 41:40-41; 55).[12] Another puzzle is the preoccupation of *SQ* with the fact of Jesus' messiahship without corresponding efforts to spell out its nature. He is a prophet. He works miracles by a word of command. He is believed in as the Messiah by those who see his miracles.

SQ may be early—whether before or after 70 CE is impossible to say—but it is not undeveloped. It is a complete gospel, although remarkably free of sayings. Of these, the Passion story has the most. There is a careful literary structure involving an itinerary. Seven stylized miracles occur in the center, the Galilean group of four introduced by a conversation with Nathanael who becomes a believer, the Judaean group of three by a conversation with another skeptic, a Samaritan woman, who does the same. The Passion narrative is not as neatly structured as the introductory materials on the Baptist (1:19-34, selectively) and the early witnesses (1:35-49) because it contains the most traditional and extensive units that go to make up *SQ*. Despite its earliness, the Passion account with its two trial stories is a developed one, not by any means a record of primitive historical tradition.

Thus, the antipathy to Jesus of the chief priests and the Temple guard, plus the Pharisees, is already taken for granted. The terminology proper to the Roman army is used of the Temple guard (18:12), a detail that may not have been inaccurate. It is assumed that priests and Pharisees together could convene the Sanhedrin (11:47*a*), a possible historical testimony to the makeup of that body. There is confusion in the tradition on the relative roles of Annas and Caiaphas, but not on the fact that the former was a person of influence. A matter-of-fact hearing before him in *SQ* (18:19-23) becomes a full-scale scene in John, followed by a second formal examination before Caiaphas. *SQ* simply sends him from one to the other, verse 13 followed by 24, with the presence of Peter at the high priest's gate, an incident at Caiaphas's house, not Annas's house as in John's Gospel. In his appearance before the high priest in *SQ* (Caiaphas, not Annas), Jesus' only exchange concerns the fact of his public teaching (18:19-23). His response is enough to have him sent to Pilate (v. 28).

SQ is almost devoid of the lively exchange between Jesus and Pilate with which we are familiar from John's Gospel. Pilate asks him if he is the king of the Jews/Judaea, hears the response, "It is you who say it," and immediately declares that he finds no cause to condemn him (vv. 33, 37, 38). The source knows of Barabbas and the Passover custom of an amnesty (vv. 39-40), of the shouts "Away with him!" and "Crucify him!" (19:15, 6), of Pilate's efforts to set Jesus free, which the threat that he may be no "Friend of Caesar" overrides, of his taking his seat on the judge's bench at the Stone Pavement—*Gabbatha* in Hebrew (19:13)—at about noon on Preparation Day, and finally of his delivering of Jesus over to be crucified (vv. 12-14*a*; 16). Interspersed between the notations of time and place and Jesus' final disposition (vv. 14*a* and 16) is the mocking scene at the hands of Roman soldiers (19:1-3) much like that of the Synoptists before the soldiery of the priests.

The general likenesses of *SQ* to the Synoptic source material, namely, Mark's B stream and Luke's Passion source, are clear. In none does Jesus' response to the priestly question about his messiahship extend beyond acknowledgment of the fact. This is taken as sufficient to have had him brought before imperial authority where, again, his neutral "You say so" (Mark 15:2) is considered nonincriminatory. In *SQ,* substitution of Barabbas for Jesus is proposed by Pilate and rejected by the crowd, and Jesus is let go to his death without his guilt having been established. It is no wonder that all four Evangelists, faced with such meager traditional material, felt that they had to flesh out the narrative if they were to be believed at all.

We are left with the puzzle of why the narratives in the early stages of their development went in the direction they did. Would primitive historical traditions account for these narratives best? Were there traditions of appearances before Jewish authority and then Roman in which Jesus made no messianic claims but took no pains to deny them, then went to his death because it was naturally concluded that this silence was guilt enough? Does the persistence of the Barabbas tradition (common to Luke's Passion source and *SQ* and classified by Taylor in Mark's B stream) tell us anything about its primitive character? Was the mockery of Jesus in the form of a game a constant in the tradition, put to use early in a variety of circumstances, and Peter's denial equally such as something based on historical reminiscence?

An affirmative answer to the above questions, with one exception, seems to be in order. That exception is the Barabbas story, which could have come to birth for apologetic reasons, apart from any historical considerations. The Gospels abound in clues that suggest the early confusion between the kind of *basileía* Jesus preached and the Zealot movement that had already taken shape in active revolt by the time the Gospels were written. Rome's condemnation of him on suspicion of being implicated in the activities of an early such movement is extremely likely. This means that believers in him, sensitive to the charge of such direct involvement from the beginning and anxious to deny it, would have taken pains to set in contrast a genuine seditionist (*lēstēs*) and Jesus, who was innocent of any such charge. The opposition thus highlighted would have been between the innocent one going to his death and the guilty one going free, with the governor fully conscious of the paradox. The only details that tell against such a construct are the occurrence of a name in all the accounts and the designation of "the uprising" as if it were well-known current history.

Could the framers of the most primitive Passion narratives have thought that their accounts would convince anyone that such was the truth of things? Yes, since Christians, for whom the Gospels were written, were convinced that Jesus' death was humanly inexplicable anyway. Yes, too, because his innocence was for them a primary datum, the only possible real reasons being the Roman fear of "stirring up the people" and the priestly antipathy to him. Yes, finally, because Pilate's consistent finding of no cause (John 18:38) in him suited an approach of disciples of Jesus to the empire that could have been developed very early if the empire continued to harass them after his death as a group suspect of insurgency.

WHAT JOHN ADDED to HIS HYPOTHETICAL SOURCE

Looking, now, to the specific additions of John to his source, we find that the exchange between Jesus and Judas together with the would-be captors at 18:5b-9 is John's composition. Verses 1-5a are ignorant of a place called Gethsemane but contain phrases like "the one who was to hand him over" (v. 2, also 5b) and reference to the general armed condition of the captors. Both of these occur in divergent Synoptic traditions. Judas is more active in the arrest in John than in the Synoptics. When Jesus says "I am" in response to his name (v. 5a), this need not have a theophanic connotation for John, that is, like that of Exodus 3:14, but may well have been part of the tradition. The exaggerated response of falling to the ground in verse 6 may be derived from Psalms 27:2 and

35:4.[13] Jesus' foreknowledge of all that would happen to him (v. 4) is a Johannine touch. So are the responses "I am he" in verses 6 and 8, repeated from verse 5. Judas is puzzlingly reintroduced in verse 5c, perhaps to ensure that he is known to be among those affected by Jesus' announcement. Verses 8b-9 are pure Johannine theology: Jesus' request that his followers be let go and his declaration of the fulfillment of his own word (cf. 17:12; 6:39; 10:28). In the original, Jesus' acknowledgment of his identity (v. 5b) was followed by Peter's impetuous lunge (vv. 10-11) and its aftermath. There do not seem to be Johannine additions in either verse, both of which contain Synoptic echoes (cf. Matt. 26:52 par. Luke 22:51; Mark 14:36 pars.)

The phrase "the Jewish guards" (18: 12) may be John's addition, but it is just as likely to have occurred in his source. The same is true of all of verse 13, whereas 14 with its "*tois Ioudaiois*" is John's reference (cf. vv. 33, 39) to those Jews whom Caiaphas had counseled that it was better that one man die than the whole people. Meantime, John uses this term, to which he so often gives a hostile connotation for the many Jews who believed in Jesus (11:45; 12:11) as a result of his resuscitation of the dead Lazarus.[14]

We have noted above John's rearrangement of materials from SQ regarding events in the high priest's house. They occur there in conjunction with Peter's denial, as in the Synoptics generally.[15] John seems to have come on them side by side, the hearing occurring before the denials, and rewoven them to achieve the effect of simultaneity.[16] The result is the creation of a full-scale appearance before Annas (18:19-23) which included Peter's first denial and another before Caiaphas (vv. 24-27) where his second and third are situated.

The phrases of verse 20, other than "I always taught in the synagogue or in the temple area," are elaborations by John on a traditional saying as in verse 21c, "See, these men know what I said." A link is needed for resumption of the narrative; this John supplies with 25a, "There was Simon Peter, standing and warming himself." He composes 28d-32[17] and fleshes out the traditional elements of a conversation with Pilate by adding, in his familiar poetic speech, verses 34-35 (with their vehement "It is your own people and the chief priests who have handed you over to me") and 36-38*b*. The latter includes Jesus' declarations that his kingdom is not of this world; that if it were, his disciples would be fighting (cf. Matt. 26:53) to keep him from being handed over to the *Ioudaiois*; and that he has come into the world not for purposes of kingship but to testify to the truth (the role of John the Baptist in 5:33; but see 3:13; 5:19; 8:23, 26, where it is proper to Jesus to tell what he has learned from his Father).

JOHN as MASTER DRAMATIST

The next evident Johannine creation is 19:4-5, 7, the third scene between Pilate and the *Ioudaioi* (18:29-32 and 38*b*-40 having been the first two). The same is true of the fourth and last scene (19:12-16). The pre-Johannine elements here are verses 6 and 12-14*a*. Like the first interrogation of Jesus by Pilate (18:33-38*a*), which was largely the work of John, the second one (19:8-11) is John's in its entirety. It contains the Evangelist's conviction that everything was under the control of providence ("unless power were given you from above," v. 11). The fear of Pilate (v. 8) and his lesser sin than that of the one "who handed me over to you" (v. 11) are typical of John's tendency to portray Pilate as all but believing in Jesus, surely not guilty of his death in the measure that the *Ioudaioi* were.

In the Synoptics the trial before Pilate happens in one place. John uses a two-stage technique, inside the praetorium and out-side it. The transition becomes clumsy in 19:12 when the mob out-side calls to Pilate within, summoning him outside. He responds almost with docility in verse 13. Jesus' silence is reminiscent of the Synoptics' report of Jesus in the presence of the Sanhedrin (Mark 14:61) and Herod (Luke 23:9). "Where do you come from?" (19:9) is a Johannine verse (9:29; cf. 2:9; 3:8), particularly with respect to the mystery of Jesus' origins.

The "after this" of 19:12*a* (cf. 6:66) identifies 19:12*a* as Johan-nine, but there are traditional elements until 14*a*. "Behold your king!" spoken to the *Ioudaioi* (14*b*) is surely John's composition, of a piece with the "Ecce homo!" (*idou ho anthrōpos*) of 19:5. The same is true of verse 16, which places the crowd solidly with the emperor, incredible in Jesus' day and even more so of believers in him later in the century who are charged with "disregarding the emperor's decrees and claiming instead that a certain Jesus is king" (Acts 17:7*b*). John adds 20*b*-21*b* to traditional materials about the place of execution and the title over the cross, a final expression of his conviction that the *Ioudaioi* resisted Jesus' claim to kingship to the end while Pilate was more than ready to allow it.

John has been called the author of a conscious design who has exhibited in his Passion narrative, "more brilliantly than anywhere else, his power of dramatic narrative."[18] This can readily be granted. He succeeds at interweaving Peter's denial and the proceedings in the high priest's house in a way Mark would have envied. The excessive mockery and abuse in the priestly ménage in the Synoptics is reduced to one sharp blow by a guard in John. He reserves the bullying tactics and the brutality that follow for the imperial soldiers on provincial assignment, a situation well known for the ennui of all conscripted regulars. John may have his Annas and Caiaphas confused (but see Luke 3:2 for another tradition incorporating the same uncertainty). He at least contents himself with having the high priest put questions "about his disciples and about his teaching" (18:19), forgoing entirely the chance to use the occasion to score a theological point about Jesus' identity. He chooses Pilate's court for this purpose.

With a rich sense of paradox, John presents Pilate as a skeptic regarding both the claims made in favor of Jesus and those made against him by his opponents, but also as friendlier to him than the traditional opponents, the *Ioudaioi*.[19] It may be that John has no intention of engaging in political propaganda to improve the condition of Christians in the empire—the easiest thing of which to accuse him—but is carrying on to the end his polemic against the *Ioudaioi*. They are probably the Evangelist's contemporaries who consider themselves *the* Jews, possibly a self-designation for them adopted by him rather than original with him. It could be they who make the paradox of Pilate attractive to John in his day. The Gentile world is drawn to belief in Jesus while those who claim to be sons of Abraham and the sole authentic disciples of Moses cry out for his condemnation (19:6, 15).

In effect, the trial narrative of John, whatever his motivations, succeeds in arousing as much sympathy for the Roman cause and antipathy to the Jewish, in the late-first-century standoff between two groups of Jews, as those of the Synoptic authors. It is a literature of advocacy like the rest. On balance, it proves to be so effective as drama that its intent as a religious literature of persuasion is lost. Jesus' elaborations before Pilate of his meaning and purpose may be the Evangelist's major concern. Nonetheless, these do not leave nearly as lasting an impression as what is taken to be the prefect's active concern for him or the crowd's active hostility toward him.

Long after the rest of the narrative is forgotten, the phrases "Crucify him" and "We have no king but Caesar"—the first from the relatively innocuous signs-source and the second not assigned to it by Fortna, who stops short at 19:15—are still ringing in Christian ears. The stage is set for a tragic drama that will play for ages.

⊕⊕⊕⊕⊕
Chapter 7

CONCLUSIONS

T he Jewish people have suffered much at the hands of Christians from the charge that "the Jews crucified Jesus."[1] This being so, it is important to try to determine whether the charge has a basis or is baseless in the only extant documentation of the events, the four Gospels and Luke's Acts of the Apostles. The prima facie evidence is that a Jewish court of some sort found him guilty on the religious count of blasphemy, that is, reviling the Name of the All-Holy, and because incapable of executing him on that charge, turned him over to civil authority as guilty of "leading the people astray," that is, in a plot of revolt against the empire. In the documents the high priest, his Temple priestly associates, and "the elders," men of influence, press aggressively for Jesus' death. The Roman official who passes sentence has paradoxically found him innocent, even after a lengthy exchange on power and kingship. He orders Jesus flogged and "turned over to their wishes." The question is, Do we have a sober history of events in the only documentation available or a semi-fictionalized account drawn up well after they occurred? Moreover, if the people of Jerusalem had no part in Jesus' death, was the Second Council of the Vatican correct to say in 1965 on the basis of history that "neither all Jews indiscriminately at that time, nor Jews today, can be charged with the crime committed during his Passion," even though "the Jewish authorities . . . pressed for the death of Christ (John 19:6)"?

This study has gone on the assumption that the first step in arriving at the meaning of the trial narratives in the Gospels is to identify the sources that lay behind them. Such attempts at identification consist in hypotheses, which by definition are not certain, about the written sources available to Mark, Luke, and John (Matthew does not seem to employ any source but Mark; the materials proper to him appear to be his composition). It has the merit of sending one behind the theological, apologetic, and polemical considerations that were at work throughout the composition of each Gospel. The drawback is that one is brought up short before a variety of sources which differ among themselves, after developments within them can be shown from the initial stage of historical reminiscence. While the theology underlying the sources is discernible, it is not so easy to name the influences that modified the historical traditions in the direction of the trial narratives as they appear in the sources.

The source criticism attempted in these pages is modest and largely derivative. It is the work of twentieth-century scholars who thought historically in the modern manner, hence envisioned each Gospel as a mosaic of previously existing materials. They were not at ease with the idea that all four authors were literary geniuses of the Jewish and Greco-Roman worlds who were more creative than constructive in their work of compilation. Words, phrases, or narratives that could not be identified as having come from a source were categorized almost dismissively as "free compositions," as if the Evangelist had deserted his primary task of depending on sources for the authenticity of his account and dared to go out on his own. What tracking sources where possible does, however, is carry us back to an earlier written stage in each of the four Gospels, without taking a stand on the various oral traditions that could have influenced them. Its hesitance to identify the free composition of the individual Evangelist Matthew is based on the inability to discuss a source. Thus, the material special to Matthew or Luke has been designated M and L, respectively, rather than Mt or Lk, while the scholarly world at times throws up its hands over how much in John is unique to him and cannot be shown to derive from a source or sources.

Nowhere in these pages does the supposition appear that, in retreating to one immediate earlier stage in Gospel composition, we have thereby come upon authentic historical traditions unaffected by any apologetic or theological concerns. Rather, it is supposed only that these sources were nearer to the historical reality than are the extant Gospels. It is further supposed that whatever is found in some form in *various* sources of the Gospels has historical likelihood on its side, although the early historicizing of certain typological and theological constructs is by no means precluded.

We may not go on the assumption that because dependability of historical detail means much to us it had the same importance for the Evangelists and their predecessors. They were greatly concerned that God had acted in history and they told of God's action in terms of human, historical activity. In fact, however, they were reporting on what they were convinced was the outworking of a providential plan foreshadowed in the Scriptures, fulfilled in terms of the conflict of good and evil. They made their report in a highly sophisticated way in the context of the religious thought of the times, but unsophisticatedly as regards the historiography of our day. They chose their villains and their heroes, except in those few instances where reliable historical reminiscence had chosen them for them. The Evangelists did not hesitate to enlist sympathy for Jesus' plight, to evoke the conviction that there had been a miscarriage of justice, or to see in the Jewish leaders agents provocateurs with respect to an oppressive imperial power whose agents they were in collecting taxes from the Jews and conveying them to Rome.

The following conclusions seem to be inescapable, once the history of the formation of the Passion narratives is seriously taken into account:

1. The Gospels are chiefly interested in presenting the death of Jesus, condemned and executed as a criminal by the Romans, as juridically inexplicable in light of his patent innocence. They see him, above all, as free of the charge that he was an insurgent against legitimate imperial authority, taking part in a Jewish liberation movement religiously inspired.

2. The Gospels in the form in which they reach us are convinced that Jewish religious leadership, specifically Temple priestly leadership, contrived the death of Jesus by having him brought to trial on political charges sufficiently persuasive to have Pilate sentence him to death. In earlier stages the narrative materials that derived from tradition were content with a summoning of Jesus to answer priestly inquiry on religious charges, both of speech against the Temple and of claims of intimacy with God. A later development was the picture of a hearing before the high priest in the house of Annas which arrived at a finding of blasphemy. This was changed on its way to Pilate to a charge of subversion in civil circumstances. There is no Gospel evidence, however, that Jesus appeared before religious authority to answer political charges.

3. Only one inference can be drawn regarding what took place during Jesus' appearance before Pilate besides that represented by the concluding phrase, "he delivered him over to them [the chief priests of the preceding verse?] to be crucified" (John 19:16). The *titulus* on the cross that Pilate ordered and would not rescind under pressure (assuming its historical character in some form since it occurs in different wording in all four Gospels) suggests that Jesus' political stance and perhaps messiahship—whatever that religious title meant to Pilate—came up at the trial. His reported spirit of unwillingness to condemn Jesus as charged, which he ultimately did anyway, and the heavy irony of calling him a king on the placarded title he authorized, may have signaled his contempt for Jewish-political power. At the same time, he may have thrown a bone in bringing about the death of Jesus to the Temple priests and Sanhedrin for the little power in that order that they wielded.

4. There is a dependable historical tradition of antipathy between Jesus and certain leaders among the Temple priests (called *archiereis*

in the Gospels) throughout his appearances in Jerusalem, including his final one. That this antipathy had a part in his death seems impossible to deny. There is the further tradition of an appearance before one or more persons highly placed in the Jerusalem community. It is variously the "high priest" (Mark 14:53), "Caiaphas" (Matt. 26:57) in "his house" (v. 58), "Annas, the father-in-law of Caiaphas" (John 18:13) and then "Caiaphas" (v. 24), and "all the chief priests, the elders, and the scribes" (Mark 14:53), identified as "the whole Sanhedrin (Matt. 26:59) and "their Sanhedrin" (Luke 22:66*b*). Although it is possible that matters like the report of a questioning, the names of the questioners, and the locale were all developed from the simple known fact of the antipathy, as was the account of what took place before the assembled council, it is more likely that the Gospels retain a core of historical tradition on a hearing before a powerful person or persons. Similarly, some exchange between them on the question of messiahship—however that term was conceived—is to be credited. The title "Son of God" *may* have arisen in this connection but its use is more likely to reflect post-Easter Christology. No other exchange is to be accorded any primitive historical character. The chief reason for accepting such a hearing as having taken place is the testimony to it in Luke's Passion source at 22:66-70, separate from and not dependent on Mark 14:60-62.

5. An important development under point 3 above is the Barabbas story. It is used in the Gospels for dramatic effect to highlight Pilate's friendly neutrality, much as Peter's personal denial is made to set in relief an official, public rejection of Jesus. Conceivably, the Barabbas tale was developed as a paradigm of the actual guilt of sedition in contrast to Jesus' innocence of the charge, much as in the case of the two thieves flanking Jesus (who have ceased to be *lēstai*, "rebels," in Luke and have become there *kakourgoi*, unspecified "malefactors"/"evildoers"). Because of the Barabbas story's persistence in the tradition, it may have some historical foundation, although probably not in the form of the festal pardon and exchange for Jesus that is reported.

6. If, as is the case in Luke and John, there is no reference to a session of the Sanhedrin in which Jesus was condemned to

death (in John there is no reference to the Sanhedrin or to a body of any sort), the question raised in point 4 above remains: Who exactly were the interrogators in the Gospels' sources and in what circumstances? They are "the Sanhedrin" and "the entire assembly" in Luke's source (22:66—23:1) and "the whole Sanhedrin" in Mark's non-Semitic A stream (15:1). Matthew, editing Mark, omits the Sanhedrin and contents himself with "all the chief priests and the elders of the people" (27:1). He consciously leaves out Mark's "scribes" as well. Luke, presumably less familiar with Jewish practice than Matthew except through sources that are historically dependable, retains "scribes" (22:66). Matthew's omission of the Sanhedrin may be owing to a sound historical sense, but also to his observation that Mark has not named that body in the "night trial" (14:54; cf. Matt. 26:57) and that to do so later (Matt. 27:1) is unnecessary.

From fairly consistent usage beginning with Jesus' confrontation over authority within the temple precincts, the three groups in opposition to him are identified as "the chief priests and the scribes and the elders" (Mark 11:27 and Luke 20:1; "scribes" omitted from Matt. 21:23, but see 26:57 for "scribes and elders"). The relatively persistent mention of this trio argues to their occurrence in the Evangelists' sources. This moves Flusser to argue for the historicity of a Temple committee made up of leading priests, senior laymen, and secretaries.[2] He finds support in the fact that the highly influential Pharisees occur only once in the Passion account (John 18:3; see also, however, Matt. 27:62), a mention that he discounts by reference to the "less historical John." Mark and Matt. have the Pharisees plotting against Jesus to entrap him in speech, for the last time in 12:13 and its parallel 22:15, respectively. Luke says that this is done to "hand him over to the office and authority of the governor" (20:20) but, probably with a careful eye to the Pharisees' nonappearance in his Passion source, he omits mention of them here in favor of "the scribes and the chief priests" (20:19).

Jesus' historical opponents, therefore, were certain of the chief priests and their associates. It is probable that they became the whole Sanhedrin in a dramatization of the story in Christian circles, although it is possible that Luke 22:66 (supported by John 18:28) has retained a historical reminiscence of an early-morning session of that body. Luke has the alignment of Jesus' last hours persisting in Acts, where the "captain of the temple guard" (4:1; 5:24, 26) who were engaged in harassing the disciples as the agent of the Sadducees, high priests, and Sanhedrin parallels the Temple guards who accompanied the chief priests to their capture of Jesus (Luke 22:52). The latter usage is found in Luke's Passion source but not in Mark. Luke's own acquaintance with the *sagan ha-kohanim* (chief officer of the priests) of the Mishnah or Josephus's *ish har habhith* (man in charge of the outer forecourt) may be presumed to be minimal, but his source reports accurately on the Levitical soldiery. He also, interestingly, possesses a tradition that mentions "Annas the high priest and Caiaphas [neither of whom appear by name in his Gospel, presumably because of their absence from his source] and John [Mark], and Alexander" as members of the inimical priestly class (Acts 4:6), and Gamaliel the Pharisee as defender of the early disciples (5:34).

7. While Pilate was expedient enough in outlook to execute Jesus, there is nothing to hinder the fact of his not having seen in him a great threat to the empire, which is another way of saying that his reported diffidence may be based on a kernel of historical truth. "Just another religious preacher of insurgency," might have been his thought, "whom the leadership here in Jerusalem wants nothing to do with."

ACKNOWLEDGING the BIASES of the GOSPELS as THEY COME to US

The Gospels are a tendentious literature, of this there can be no doubt. If they were simply an intramural literature like the five books of Moses or the writings of the prophets, they would have had another fate. Like those earlier examples, they were composed by Jews who were committed to reform within the faith community of Israel. Unlike them, they were written in a language the Gentile could understand and not in the ancient Hebrew tongue of the fathers. They might even have been composed in the hope that Gentile nonbelievers in Jesus would read them, but that is unlikely. Like the books of the Old Testament, they are a Community's Faith Literature.

An important difference was that, whatever the divisions in Israel of the past (as, for example, between northern and southern kingdoms, collaborators and separatists, royalty and priesthood, priesthood and laity), the concept of peoplehood had remained fairly firm throughout all division in Israel. The Qumran documents, despite their testimony to religious schism, tell of schism within a people. The New Testament writings, likewise compositions by, and largely for, the Jewish people, were marked by this difference: they were also addressed to Jewish proselytes (Gentile males who had accepted circumcision and with it the whole Law) and to the much larger number of "God-fearers," the pious Gentiles who allied themselves with Israel but did not go that far in Law observance, and to any Greek-speaking Gentiles who might hear these writings recited publicly. This literature went on the assumption, in other words, that the universalist hope of the prophets like Isaiah (see 56:6-7; 66:18, 23) was a present reality, or could be. It stood for eschatology now, the last days already inaugurated and upon us.

The Jewish faith community of the period, after the fall of Jerusalem in particular, generally resisted what had been the widespread assumption, of God's imminent inbreaking to do perfect justice for an oppressed people. The rabbis began to urge this people to abandon dreams of an imminent end time and live lives faithful to the Law. With the gospel an invitation was being extended to it to cling to the hope, even more to depart from almost two millennia of history as a people just at the point when solidarity in peoplehood had been given fresh impetus by the siege of the Romans of city and Temple. The effect was a deep division, not only along linguistic, ethnic, and cultural lines but along faith lines as well. The New Testament contains testimony to this division—one that is broader, surely, by the time the Gospels and Acts were written than at the time of the formation of the first written fragments of historical tradition.

It has been demonstrated in these pages that the tensions between the Jews who believed in Jesus and those who did not brought about a radical alteration in the religious literature produced by the former. The writings went from the relatively colorless earliest narratives we can reconstruct to their present dramatized form, full of conversations, reported utterances of Jesus, and devices intended to sway the reader. Their earlier development can only be guessed at. The Gospels are a faith literature like the Bible and like the Bible they bristle with antipathies, identifying the enemies of the authors with the enemies of God. An important difference is that the Evangelists are believers who have taken on new enemies, "the scribes and Pharisees" or "the Jews," much in the manner of "the priests and prophets" of Jeremiah's day or "the church" for contemporary Christians who mean the church's leadership.

The deep division between Jews who believed in Jesus' resurrection and the other Jews to whom they proclaimed it made some sense for the first forty years after Jesus' death. It was the kind of thing that Israel had been through many times before. But after the destruction of Jerusalem in 70 and after the formation of the academy at Iavneh (Jamnia) some time around 85, in effect a slow replacement of the Sanhedrin, everything began to be changed. For Jews the religion of Israel gradually became Judaism by the rabbis' defining how the written and oral Law should be kept. This had not been the case heretofore. And they spoke of the assembled Jewish people as the synagogue. Concurrently, some Jews of the diaspora, along with God-fearers and Gentiles who believed in Christ risen, began to call themselves *ekklēsia* translating *qahal*, "assembly" or "church." The "Jews" became for these mixed Jewish–Gentile communities the religious-establishment figures under whom they had previously fretted in Roman Palestine as the despised, as "the people of the land" who did not know the Law. These mixed communities began to be called in some second-century sources *christianism,* identical in suffix with *Judaism.* Only by the year 200 were the groups fully distinguished, but the seeds of antipathy had been sown from one side in the Gospels and Epistles. No written record remains of the rabbinic response. There is no comparable Jewish literature from the period, probably because the sect was deemed beneath notice.

What this means is that the writings of Christians on their origins made religious sense within Christian circles before 100 but slowly began to make less sense as Jewish literature because so many Gentiles had come to espouse the gospel. The Passion narratives, with their appeal to the emotions and their facile alignments of the main actors, are among the writings that widened the breach between church and synagogue. The chief perpetrators of Jesus' death continued to be, in Christian eyes, a coalition of forces marked by ill will: "Herod and Pontius Pilate in league with the Gentiles and the peoples of Israel," in an early prayer placed on the lips of Peter and John, "have brought about the very things which in your powerful providence you planned long ago" (Acts 4:27-28, following 25b-26, an exact quotation from the LXX of Psalm 2:1 on the rage of the kings of earth against the LORD and his Anointed).[3] But this global guilt in a providential context was soon forgotten. It yielded to accounts not only of the guilt of the priestly leadership but its sentencing of Jesus to death in solemn conclave on a charge of blasphemy. It gave place to a narrative of Pilate as a philosophically minded person who scarcely seemed to have a part in any judicial proceedings against Jesus.

It is the responsibility of Christians to get behind the trial accounts to their basic faith commitment that the death of Jesus was caused by the sins of men. An important step in this progress is to identify the unhistorical as unhistorical in the way that modern critical scholarship is peculiarly fitted to do.

It is not helpful to replace the mythologies of the inspired authors with new mythologies, however well-intentioned the motivation. Among these replacements have been the attempt to make the Romans the devils in the piece in as uncritical a fashion as the Gospels make "the Jews," or to portray Jesus as a patriot from the north who comes to Jerusalem inciting to violence, or to maintain that the Gospels are totally worthless as clues to history.

Through all such misguided efforts the last state of the case is worse than the first.

The man Jesus was dispatched in quite unusual circumstances in an age given to violence. We should not shrink from the harsh realities that attended this particular event. What exactly they were is hard to discover. Only a small portion of the data is recoverable. When recovered it will not redound to the credit of the band of threatened men of both nations, Israel and Rome, who saw to his judicial murder. In the interests of truth every effort should be made to recover the core of the historically verifiable. This effort must be made, lest we despair of the search, as Pilate's question to Jesus—"What is truth?"—unhistorical but no less important for that—seems to have done.

CAN GOSPEL SCHOLARSHIP REDUCE CHRISTIAN ANTI-SEMITISM?

Would the tensions between Jews and Christians be lessened if the Catholic, Orthodox, and Protestant churches of every stripe were to promulgate the findings of this study long and loud, continuing to do so at every turn? Probably not. For some, critical study of the Bible is anathema. For those communions in which it is not, the popular conviction of clergy and laity is deep-seated that in the four Gospels and early Acts we have a dependable chronicle of the events that led to, and culminated in, Jesus' crucifixion.

The chief finding of these pages is that there were early clear reminiscences among Jesus' disciples of both sexes that two power blocs, Temple and empire, conspired to eliminate Jesus, each from a slightly different motive. No one among believers in his upraising from the dead had access to the deliberations and decisions of either juridical body. They did know the outcomes and in their reconstructions of the core verbal exchanges they were probably not too far off the mark. An important detail is that those who knew him in life began to have a new and quite different faith in him with his resurrection. This faith altered notably the character of the reconstructed accounts of his last days and hours.

Even if that were to be made clear many times over in all the Christian assemblies of the world, there is one remembered fact that will not go away. The Temple priestly complicity in Jesus' death seems to be as much a fact as the Roman sentence. Jesus' early disciples, all Jews, had no reason to fabricate it out of whole cloth. Jews are quite used to acknowledging the villainous, treacherous, cowardly, and venal behavior of some among them, but not in this matter. They have suffered too much over the false charge of corporate guilt for Jesus' death. Pinpointing the apparent role of priests and elders suspicious of the popularity of a fellow Jew with the mainly Galilean crowds, and furious at his teaching about the destruction of the Temple even if it was end-time prophetic in character, would provide modern Jews no relief whatever. Critical scholarship seems to be of no use in reducing Christian–Jewish tensions. Or is it?

If the Gospels and Acts were taught in the formation of preachers and Christian educators as the kind of writing that they are, that would accomplish much. But again, little is to be hoped for on that front. A defective theology of human redemption is all but universal. It is not easily reversed, nor is a better reading of the Christian mystery put in its place. The distortion of the church's faith in possession is that the remission of humanity's sinfulness and the accompanying fear of death were accomplished by the details of Jesus' sufferings and the mode of his death rather than *by his acceptance of death,* the universal human lot, *and by his resurrection from the dead by the power of God.*

The Evangelists were all too successful in their portrayal of an innocent just one who went to his death in brutal circumstances, restrained as each was in describing it. Their accounts led to the key words used by Paul and other early writers: "death," "blood," "was crucified." The public prayer forms (liturgies) of East and West stopped there, giving way in the medieval West after the year 1000 to shedding of rivers of ruddy gore in Christian preaching, art, and lately film.[4] The Reformation did nothing to stem the tide, but if anything increased the flow. *Das Kreuz Jesu* and faith in its efficacy became the sole instrument of human salvation, his resurrection a divine vindication of his innocence. To say this is not to say that physical pain and mental anguish had no part in the divine drama. They were in every sense the coin of human redemption. But, in this metaphor, the circumstances of Jesus' obedient death have been allowed to overshadow the basic reality. To call Jesus' death obedient is to describe the passage from life of one who, by all accounts, could have escaped not the universal fate but the ignominy of his departure from life. St. Paul rightly calls death "the last enemy." Only by having countered death through having been raised up from it could Jesus be said to have vanquished humanity's common enemy. Enduring the terrible torture and pain that so many fellow humans have experienced was not that by which he became, for believers in him, "the savior of the world." It was the spirit in which he lived and died, one of perfect openness to the divine will.

The dramatic character of Jesus' exit from life has spawned a multitude of Good Friday *tre ore* sermons, a host of Passion plays, novels and novellas, devotion to the five wounds, the sacred side, and the sacred shoulder, not to speak of the devotion known as the stations of the cross, and hour-long sermons on Jesus' sufferings. If good preaching on the mystery of Calvary is fated to be the minority situation, what is to be hoped for in reducing Jewish–Christian tensions from a scholarly inquiry like the present one? Much, in every respect.

If such study were to be engaged in seriously not only by pastors and other preachers but by religion teachers and the producers of catechetical (read Christian education) materials, much would be accomplished. But much more would be done if agencies charged with the public prayer life of the churches—bishops for the communions that have them, the worship commissions of middle judicatories, any persons charged with the order of service in local congregations—were to keep a careful eye out for the lyrics of hymns, sermon aids for preachers, and above all the reading of a lengthy Gospel Passion narrative on Palm Sunday or Good Friday. There still live in the United States and Canada the descendants of European Jews who have learned that their parents or grandparents stayed behind bolted doors on Good Friday in fear of marauding bands of toughs. The thugs were often illiterate. What they heard in church or catechism class gave them what they thought was a free pass to thuggery.

The Roman Catholic Church of the West lost a great opportunity when, in proposing a three-year cycle of Bible readings from both Testaments called *Lectionary for Mass,* it retained the practice from the early Middle Ages of reading a long Passion narrative on Palm Sunday and Good Friday. It was always Matthew in the former instance and John in the latter. There was a change to Matthew, Mark, and Luke on the Sundays of successive years and the suggestion that the early portions of each reading of two chapters could be abbreviated or even omitted. The *Revised Common Lectionary* continued the practice. The celebration of Jesus' entry into Jerusalem on the borrowed foal of an ass was in effect submerged and Holy Week was launched as a long Good Friday to the obscuring of the paschal three days.

The real harm that continues to be done consists in the natural supposition of worshipers that they are hearing historical chronicles correct in every detail. What they are hearing is Semitic stories told by Semitic storytellers adept at multiplied metaphor and the interspersion of snatches from scripture as fulfillments of ancient prophecy. Hearers are understandably led to believe that they are privy to what the high priest, Pilate, Peter, and Jesus said, each in his exact words. A dramatic reading by three readers at lecterns is undoubtedly interesting because the story in interesting. Far more interesting and, more importantly, faith-nourishing would be a short selection from each Synoptic Gospel on Monday, Tuesday, and Wednesday every year and a homily or sermon in exposition of how the individual Evangelists created a faith literature from their already theologically developed sources. A book like the present one could provide immense help in this. Any Catholic presider at weekday evening Masses or Protestant leader in Bible study is free to do this and, above all, at the Good Friday communion service with John as well. For those who think they experience no such freedom on Palm Sunday, a seven-minute prior instruction on what to listen for and what not to believe as historical fact will do. There should not be a stopping at Jesus' entombment but always a proceeding to an account of the empty tomb and his risen state, however brief. For if the paschal three days are erroneously to be anticipated on Palm Sunday it ought to be in terms of the whole mystery of redemption, not the truncated portion of it.

⊕⊕⊕⊕⊕⊕

NOTES

CHAPTER 1–SCHOLARSHIP REGARDING JESUS' SENTENCE to DEATH

1. Important studies have been those of Hans Lietzmann (1931), G. D. Kilpatrick (1953), and Paul Winter (1961). Ernst Bammel edited some important essays in honor of C. F. D. Moule, conservative in the spirit of the man they honor: *The Trial of Jesus,* Studies in Biblical Theology 2/13 (1970). See also the symposium, "The Trial of Jesus in the Light of History," in *Judaism* 20 (1971): 6–74, which contains articles by H. Cohn, M. S. Enslin, D. Flusser, R. M. Grant, S. G. F. Brandon, J. Blinzler, S. Sandmel, and the present writer; Werner H. Kelber, ed., *The Passion in Mark: Studies on Mark 14–16* (Philadelphia: Fortress Press, 1976); see also David R. Catchpole, *The Trial of Jesus: A Study in the Gospels and Jewish Historiography from 1770 to the Present Day,* Studia Post-Biblica 18 (Leiden: Brill, 1971). Most important of all is Raymond E. Brown, *The Death of the Messiah: From Gethsemane to the Grave: A Commentary on the Passion Narratives in the Four Gospels,* 2 vols. (New York: Doubleday, 1994), which examines each passage in painstaking detail.

2. In a well-argued, brief essay, Robert M. Grant holds that in the light of history, responsibility for Jesus' death "belongs to those who had the responsibility of maintaining the peace in a frontier province of the Roman empire,"

though he allows collaboration by "the Sadducean high priest and his family . . . in getting rid of a potentially revolutionary leader." "The Trial of Jesus in the Light of History," *Judaism* 20 (1971): 42. On the proper title for Pilate, see J. Vardeman, "A New Inscription Which Mentions Pilate as Prefect," *JBL* 81 (1962): 70–71; also Jack Finegan, *The Archaeology of the New Testament* (Princeton: Princeton University Press, 1969), 79–80; cf. Antonio Frova, "L'iscrizione di Ponzio Pilato a Caesarea," *Rendiconti dell' Istituto Lombardo* 95 (1961): 419–34, which reports on an important archaeological discovery.

3. Mark 15:8 speaks of the "crowd" pressing its demand on Pilate for a prisoner's release, the "chief priests" at the same time inciting the crowd to have him release Barabbas instead of Jesus (v. 11). The chief priests and the "elders" do the convincing of the crowd in Matthew 27:20. The "entire assemblage" leads Jesus before Pilate in Luke 23:1, becoming the "chief priests and the crowds" in v. 4, the "chief priests and the scribes" as accusers in v. 10, and "the chief priests, the rulers, and the people" in v. 13. In John 18:31 and 38, Pilate is in exchange simply with the "*Ioudaioi*" over what to do with Jesus. Which Evangelist, if any, is correct?

4. The Gospels claim this Jewish motivation; therefore, on historical grounds it can be held to be the case. But it is more likely to be a matter of Christian conviction on erroneously conceived doctrinal grounds. For extensive documentation of the Christian sense that Jewish guilt with respect to the death of Jesus has for long been part of Christian faith commitment, see Jules Isaac, *Jesus and Israel* (New York: Holt, Rinehart and Winston, 1971). Early Christian authors post–70 CE, such as Barnabas, Justin, Tertullian, and Origen, named the destruction of Jerusalem as a punishment of the Jews for the death of Jesus, even as certain rabbis connected it with the persecution of the prophets by the fathers, failure to keep the Sabbath, and other, similar moral lapses. See Gerard S. Sloyan, *The Crucifixion of Jesus: History, Myth, Faith* (Minneapolis: Fortress Press, 1995), esp. chap. 3, "Patristic Attribution of Jesus' Death to the Jews," 72–97. Those who favor the authenticity of 1 Thes 2:14ff. say that it is part and parcel of scientific openness to take hard polemical texts like this one seriously, knowing of the "freedom that allows us to take a new road beyond the things of the past." Such is Otto Michel's view, cited by John M. Oesterreicher, "Deicide as a Theological Problem," in *Brothers in Hope, "The Bridge,"* vol. 5 (New York: Herder & Herder, 1970), 199–200. Note the important declaration of the Second Vatican Council, 28 October 1965, *Nostra Aetate* 4 ("In Our Day"), that "neither all Jews indiscriminately at that time, nor Jews today, can be charged with the crimes committed during Christ's passion." This total exculpation of Jewish guilt by Christians, a first in twenty centuries, was preceded in 1964, 1948, and 1961 by World Council of Churches statements,

by those of three regional Protestant bodies, and followed by many, Catholic and Protestant, deploring anti-Semitism in all its forms, with the accusation of responsibility for Jesus' death at its core. See also Eugene J. Fisher and Leon Klenicki, eds., *In Our Time: The Flowering of Jewish-Catholic Dialogue* (Mahwah, N.J.: Stimulus, 1990), which includes Vatican documents of 1974 and 1985; Helga Croner, compiler, *Stepping Stones to Further Jewish–Christian Relations: An Unabridged Collection of Christian Documents* (Mahwah, N.J.: Stimulus, 1977).

5. Samuel Sandmel, "The Trial of Jesus: Reservations," *Judaism* 20 (1971): 71.

6. Ibid., 73.

7. Haim H. Cohn, *The Trial and Death of Jesus* (New York: Harper & Row, 1971).

8. Haim H. Cohn, "Reflections on the Trial of Jesus," *Judaism* 20 (1971): 18–19.

9. Ibid., 20.

10. Ibid., 22.

11. They are (1) *Baraita Sanhedrin* 43*a*; (2) *Baraita Sanhedrin* 67*a*, Eng. trans. in *The Babylonian Talmud*, ed. I. Epstein, *Seder Nezikin V, Sanhedrin*, vol. 1 (London: Soncino, 1935), 281–82 and 456, n. 5; (3) *Mishnah Aboth* 1, 6, about a "Jesus" (of Nazareth?) who was a disciple of Joshua ben Perahyah; for *Aboth* 1, 6, see *Nezikin VIII, Aboth* (London: Soncino, 1935), 5; R. Travers Herford, *The Ethics of the Talmud: Sayings of the Fathers* (repr., New York: Schocken, 1962), 26–27; for discussion of the specific *baraita*, see Joseph Klausner, *Jesus of Nazareth: His Life, Times, and Teachings* (London: George Allen & Unwin, 1929), 24–26; Klausner takes up the two passages mentioned from *Sanhedrin* on 27–28 and 21–22, respectively.

12. S. G. F. Brandon, *The Trial of Jesus of Nazareth* (New York: Stein and Day, 1968), 150; see also his positions in chap. 3, n. 34, below. Martin Hengel, author of *Die Zeloten* (Leiden: Brill, 1961), maintains in *Was Jesus a Revolutionist?* (Minneapolis: Fortress Press, 1971), 34, that the available data by no means reveal Jesus as a revolutionist in the current political sense, although he was a superlative one in teaching inner freedom from the powers of the world—a quite different matter.

13. Sandmel, "Trial," 73.

14. Ibid., 72.

15. On this see Emilio G. Chavez, *The Theological Significance of Jesus' Temple Action in Mark's Gospel* (Lewiston, N.Y.: Edwin Mellen, 2002).

16. Cf. the seven kinds of Pharisees listed in *Berakoth* 14*b*, of which the first five are hypocrites (e.g., "the shoulder-Pharisee who lays commandments on men's shoulders"), and the last two upright types; recall as well

the death of Alexander Janneus, the Sadducean king (died 78 BCE), who warned his wife not against true Pharisees but against the "painted ones, whose deeds are the deeds of Zimri, but who expect to receive the reward of Phinehas," *Sota 22b*. The reference to Phinehas is to Numbers 25:6-15.

17. An exception occurs after the trial proper in Matthew 27:62 (the setting of guards at Jesus' tomb), which seems to be a later legendary accretion. John 11:47 does set the Pharisees side by side with the chief priests in assembling the Sanhedrin while in 18:3 this combination was behind the soldiery that apprehended Jesus. This may be the result of later editorial activity. On this, see Paul Winter, *On the Trial of Jesus*, Studia Judaica 1, 2d rev. ed. (Berlin: de Gruyter, 1974), 64-67.

18. For a summary of the conviction arrived at through his researches that apologetic motifs prevailed in the trial narratives, see Paul Winter, "Zum Prozess Jesu," in K. G. Eckert et al., *Antijudaismus im Neuen Testament? Exegetische und systematische Beiträge* (Munich: Chr. Kaiser, 1967), 103.

19. Good discussions of the theological presuppositions that guided the four Evangelists in their choice of traditional materials, ordering of events, and emphases are found in Howard Clark Kee, *Jesus in History: An Approach to the Study of the Gospels* (New York: Harcourt, Brace & World, 1970), and notably in "C. The Role of Theology," Jesus' own theology and the Passion theology of each Evangelist, in Brown, *Death of the Messiah*, 1:24–35.

CHAPTER 2—WHAT ROMAN LAW ALLOWED

1. 1 Cor. 1:23; 2:2.

2. Acts 2:23; 4:28; chap. 7, esp. vv. 52-53; 8:32-35. The first and last are the more circumspect. Others in between do not hesitate to accuse Jesus' contemporaries of conducting themselves murderously, as their fathers had done with the prophets. An exception is constituted by 3:17, which has Peter saying that the people and their rulers acted "in ignorance." The saying contained in many later manuscripts of Luke's Gospel, "Father, forgive them, for they know not what they do" (23:34), expresses this same outlook. Acts 13:27 takes the harder line, 17:30 the softer one. Acts chapter 3, v. 15 contains an indictment of the population of Jerusalem and v. 17 an exoneration. Ernst Haenchen, *The Acts of the Apostles: A Commentary* (Philadelphia: Westminster, 1971), 207, n. 3, suggests that Luke was not the first to introduce this mitigation (cf. Lev. 22:14; Num. 15:22-31, which speak of infringement of Law through inadvertence) but received it from tradition.

3. A midrash is a composition that explains the Hebrew Scriptures and tries to make them understandable and meaningful for a later generation. Two forms it can take are the homiletic adaptation of a text and a rewritten

version of the biblical narrative. The Passion accounts, with their copious dependence on biblical writings, have numerous midrashic elements of the type *haggadah* (that is, "tradition" or "narrative," as contrasted with *halakah,* "way" or "ethical teaching").

4. Josephus, *Jewish War* 2.117 (2.8.1).

5. Josephus, *Antiquities* 8.2 (18.1.1).

6. Cf. Robert M. Grant, *Augustus to Constantine: The Rise and Triumph of Christianity in the Roman World* (New York: Harper & Row, 1970), 28–29. Josephus lists two confrontations with the Jews, one over images of Caesar smuggled into Jerusalem by night and the other over using the Temple treasury (*corbonas*) to build an aqueduct (*Jewish War* 2.169–77 [2.9.2-4]; cf. Philo, *Legation to Gaius,* 276–78).

7. *Ant.* 18.63-64 (18.3.3). For scholars who favor the genuineness of the text, see Louis H. Feldman, in his trans., *Josephus,* vol. 9 (Cambridge: Harvard University Press, 1965), 48–49, 573–75; also S. G. F. Brandon, *Jesus and the Zealots: A Study of the Political Factor in Primitive Christianity* (Manchester: Manchester University Press, 1967), 361, n. 1. The passage occurs in the Greek text of Josephus, but the bracketed phrase does not occur in the shorter, tenth-century Arabic text of Bishop Agapius, quoted in his *Book of History Guided by All the Virtues of Wisdom,* as reported in the Shlomo Pines's monograph *An Arabic Version of the Testimonium Flavianum and Its Implications,* (Jerusalem: Israeli Academy of Sciences and Humanities, 1971). John P. Meier proposes this reconstruction of the text as Josephus may have written it: "At this time there appeared Jesus, a wise man. For he was a doer of startling deeds, a teacher of people who received the truth with pleasure. And he gained a following both of many Jews and many of Greek origin. And when Pilate, because of an accusation made by the leading men among us, condemned him to the cross, those who had loved him previously did not cease to do so. And up until this very day the tribe of Christians (named after him) has not yet died out." *A Marginal Jew: Rethinking the Historical Jesus,* vol. 1 (New York: Doubleday, 1991), 61. See pp. 59–68 with endnotes.

8. See A. N. Sherwin-White, *Roman Society and Roman Law in the New Testament* (Oxford: Clarendon, 1963), 12.

9. J. Vardeman, "A New Inscription Which Mentions Pilate as Prefect," *JBL* 81 (1962): 70–71; also Jack Finegan, *The Archaeology of the New Testament* (Princeton: Princeton University Press, 1969), 79–80; cf. Antonio Frova, "L'iscrizione di Ponzio Pilato a Caesarea," *Rendiconti dell' Istituto Lombardo* 95 (1961): 419–34.

10. *Annales* 15.44.

11. Cf. Matt. 27:2, 11, 15, 21, 27; John 18:28 through 19:38 passim.

12. Cf. Matt. 20:8; Luke 8:3.

13. *Ant.* 18.33 (18.2.2); but for the *epítropos* of the Claudian period, cf. 20.99 (20.5.1).

14. Cf. Sherwin-White, *Roman Society*, 3, 4–5, 8; also notes 4 and 5 above.

15. Cf. ibid., 12; these three powers are named as the distinguishing features of the post of administrator provincial. In support of them are cited Caesar, *Gallic Wars* 2.1.3; 5.41.5; 7.77.14–16; Velleius, 2.37.5; 117.3–4.

16. Cf. Sherwin-White, *Roman Society*, 4, 5, 9, quoting *Digesta iuris Romani*, i. 16, 6; i. 18.8–9 in *Corpus Iuris Civilis*, and Theodor Mommsen in the French edition of *Römisches Staatsrecht, Le droit publique romain*, trans. P. F. Girard (Paris: Thorin et Fils, 1893), 3:280–81.

17. Cf. Sherwin-White, *Roman Society*, 13.

18. Ibid., 16.

19. Cf. Ibid., 17.

20. Cf. notes 4 and 6 above and chap. 6, n. 17 below; Josephus's phrase is that he was "entrusted by Caesar [Augustus] with full powers including the infliction of capital punishment" (*Jewish War* 2.117 [2.8.1]). That the Roman governor would have reserved capital jurisdiction to himself to the exclusion of the Sanhedrin is, of course, the question raised by John 18:31. There is no clear evidence of Jewish practice in this matter, except the doubtful historical testimony of Acts 6:12; 7:1, 58. G. R. Driver, "The Number of the Beast," in *Bibel und Qumrân*, ed. Siegfried Wagner (Berlin: Evangelische Haupt–Bibelgesellschaft, 1968), 75, argues that the Damascus Zadokite Document (CD–A, col. IX, 1), "Every man who gives another over to anathema [that is, dooms him] shall be executed according the laws of the gentiles," reflects Coponius's taking from the Sanhedrin "the right of execution . . . for all but certain religious offences." Text not from Driver but from Florentino García Martínez, *The Dead Sea Scrolls Translated: The Qumran Texts in English*, 2d ed. (Leiden: E. J. Brill, 1996), 40.

21. Josephus, *Jewish War* 2.169–74 (2.2–3) and *Ant.* 18. 55–59 (18.3.1): *Jewish War* 2.175–77 (2.4) and *Ant.* 18.62 (18.3.2).

22. Cf. Sherwin-White, *Roman Society*, 8.

23. *Digesta iuris Romani*, i. 19. 3 in *Corpus Iuris Civilis*; F. F. Abbot and A. C. Johnson, *Municipal Administration in the Roman Empire* (Princeton: Princeton University Press, 1926), no. 58, who cite a document from Sardinia in 67 CE which says that in that territory, which also went under the rule of prefects in 6 CE, the equestrian governor's jurisdiction equaled that of the proconsul. Cf. Sherwin-White, *Roman Society*, 9, 7.

24. Cf. Mommsen, *Droit publique*, 3: 280–81.

25. *Annales* 12.60.

26. *Digesta iuris Romani*, 1.17.1.

27. On our inability to identify the circumstances of this happening, and the many who have nonetheless done so, see Paul Winter, *On the Trial of Jesus,* Studia Judaica 1, 2d. rev. ed. (Berlin: de Gruyter, 1974), 74ff. with notes 8 and 9; F. F. Bruce, *New Testament History* (Garden City, N.Y.: Doubleday Anchor Books, 1972), 36–37.

28. Cf. n. 6 above. Philo's description of him cited there is of a man "inflexible of disposition, harsh, and obdurate" (*Legation to Gaius,* 301). Philo probably never heard of Jesus.

29. *Ant.* 18.85–89 (18.4.1–2).

30. *Legation to Gaius,* 301.

31. Winter, *Trial,* 72.

32. Ibid., 55.

33. Ibid. Cf. W. G. Kümmel, *Introduction to the New Testament,* 14th rev. ed., 1965 (New York: Abingdon, 1966), who says that there is no doubt that there is a political apologetic in Luke "which fully absolves the Romans of the guilt in Jesus' crucifixion (Pilate does not condemn Jesus [23:25 against Mk. 15:15 par. Mt. 27:26]) and therewith prepares the defense of the Christians against political accusation in Acts (e.g., Acts 17:7 . . .)," 99. This assumption has to do with Luke in his day. Whatever relevance it may have had to an event of sixty years before we cannot know.

34. Brandon, *Jesus and the Zealots,* 261.

35. Ibid., 262.

36. Ibid.; cf. also 225.

37. Ibid., 262.

38. Rudolf Bultmann, *The History of the Synoptic Tradition* (German, 1921), Eng. trans. by John Marsh. 2d ed. (New York: Harper & Row; Oxford: Basil Blackwell, 1968), 270.

39. Ibid., 279 (the italics are in the original).

40. Ibid., 270.

41. Ibid., 279.

42. Ibid., cf. 272–73; but note the qualification by Bultmann about Luke 22:66 in the "Comments and Supplementary Notes," in the Eng. trans. 438 (on 272, citing J. Finegan) and 440 (on 280: Luke had no other source besides Mark). For the view that these four verses derive not from an edited version of Mark but from a special Passion source, cf. chap. 5 below.

43. *The Gospel of John: A Commentary* (German, 1941), trans. G. R. Beasley-Murray with R. W. N. Hoare and J. K. Riches (Philadelphia: Westminster; Oxford: Basil Blackwell, 1971), 648.

44. Ibid., 650.

45. Ibid., 656, n. 2.

46. Ibid., 657. The bizarre spelling "Barrabas" occurs four times on this page in the improved English translation of Beasley-Murray and

others over that of Marsh and is literally inexplicable. No manuscript witness supports it. Bultmann evidently devised it for reasons of his own.

47. Ibid., 660.

48. Cf. *Oholoth* 18.7, 9 in the Mishnah (Danby trans., 675) and *The Babylonian Talmud* ed. I. Epstein, *Seder Nezikin V, Sanhedrin*, vol. 1 (London: Soncino, 1935); *Seder Tohoroth,* trans. H. Bornstein (1948), 226; also A. Büchler, "The Levitical Impurity of the Gentile in Palestine before the Year 70," *Jewish Quarterly Review* 17 (1926–27): 1–81.

49. Cf. 2 Chronicles 7:3 in the LXX (2 Paralipomenon), where the pavement of Solomon's temple is so designated.

50. *Jewish War* 5.51 (5.2.1). Gibeah, the home place of Saul (1 Sam. 10:10, 26), is the word for hill in modern Hebrew, as Knock is in Irish, ancestral home of the present writer in County Mayo.

51. See above, p. 8. Cf. Ernest Bammel, *"Philos tou Kaisaros," Theologische Literaturzeitung* 77 (1952): 205–10. The Philo reference is to *Flaccus* 6.40.

52. *Jewish War* 2.301 (2.14.8). The passage reads: "Florus lodged at the palace, and on the following day had a tribunal placed in the front of the building and took his seat."

53. L. H. Vincent, "Chronique: L'Antonia et le Prétoire," *RB* 42 (1933): 83–113.

54. Cf. M. Aline de Sion, *La Forteresse Antonia et la question du prétoire à Jérusalem* (Jerusalem: Ex typis PP. Fransiscalium, 1955). Sorbonne thesis.

55. See the extended note of Raymond E. Brown in *The Gospel according to John (13–21),* Anchor Bible 29A (Garden City, N.Y.: Doubleday, 1970), 845; Finegan, *Archaeology,* 156–61.

56. Pierre Benoit, "Prétoire, Lithostrôton et Gabbatha," *Exégèse et Théologie,* vol. 1 (Paris: Les Éditions du Cerf, 1961), 316–39, reprinted from *RB* 59 (1952): 531–50, strongly favors Herod's palace as the site of Pilate's permanent headquarters and judgment seat. The inability to excavate it creates difficulties, but Benoit is convinced that references to it in Josephus and Philo describe it as the normal, fixed site. The Gospel data require an open space before it, which the palace had (stone pavements like that unearthed near the Antonia were not unique); it also was built on a height in the western part of the city, which satisfies Benoit's requirement for the root *gab,* a "back," "hump," or "projection." Benoit adds to the arguments for his view, in *The Passion and Resurrection of Jesus Christ* (New York: Herder & Herder, 1969), 149, n. 1, an even greater emphasis on Lithostrotos as a pavement of colored stone, and the suggestion that the rival pavement at the Sion Convent dates from the time of Hadrian (117–38).

CHAPTER 3—The INTERROGATION and TRIAL according to MARK

1. See R. H. Lightfoot, *The Gospel Message of St. Mark* (Oxford: Clarendon, 1958); Rudolf Bultmann, *The History of the Synoptic Tradition* (German, 1921), Eng. trans. by John Marsh. 2d ed. (New York: Harper & Row; Oxford: Basil Blackwell, 1968); Willi Marxsen, *Mark the Evangelist: Studies on the Redaction History of the Gospel*; Eduard Schweizer, *The Good News according to Mark: A Commentary on the Gospel*. Even if one should opt for the priority of Matthew, rather than of Mark, as a few do, it makes little difference in the Passion section, since Mark and Matthew follow basically the same lines of development, compared with the rather different accounts in Luke and John. For more recent scholarship on the Passion see John R. Donahue and Daniel J. Harrington, *The Gospel of Mark*, Sacra Pagina (Collegeville, Minn.: Liturgical Press, 2002), 401–53; Francis J. Moloney, *The Gospel of Mark: A Commentary* (Peabody, MA: Hendrickson, 2004), 297–316.

2. See W. G. Kümmel, *Introduction to the New Testament*, 14th rev. ed., (New York and Nashville: Abingdon, 1966), for a discussion of the *Ur-Markus* theories of von Soden, Wendling, and Bussmann; cf. Vincent Taylor, *The Gospel according to St. Mark*, (London: Macmillan, 1955), who concludes with the opinion that whereas a sayings source might have preceded Mark, no gospel, properly speaking, did so; also on Mark's sources, including the likelihood of a Passion source, Howard Clark Kee, *Jesus in History: An Approach to the Study of the Gospels* (New York: Harcourt, Brace & World, 1970). The most detailed and up-to-date study of these matters is Robert H. Gundry, *Mark: A Commentary on His Apology for the Cross* (Grand Rapids: Eerdmans, 1993), 853–988.

3. Distinctly Mark's, for example, are the linking words between separate passages ("and," "again," "from there," "in those days," "going from that place"); the transitional summaries (1:14-15; 3:7-12; 6:6*b*); and an occasional narrative (8:23-26; 10:46-52) or introduction (13:1-5*a*; 14:1-2, 10-12) to achieve a transition. He is also responsible for identifying Galilee as the place of Jesus' activity (1:9, 14, 16, 28, 39; 3:7; 9:30; 14:28) and as the starting point of the church's mission to the Gentiles immediately beyond the confines of Galilee (7:24, 28, 37; 13:10; 14:28). Conversely, Jerusalem is where Jesus will be handed over to suffer and to die (8:31; 9:31; 10:33; 12:12; 14:41; 15:38).

Mark concentrates material on Jesus as Christ and Savior in the second half of his Gospel (from 8:37 onward) and presents his traditional material in accord with a pattern of concealment of Jesus' identity that is not entirely clear. Some have seen in it Mark's attempt to combat a Christology of Jesus as a wonder-worker only. The disciples are a chosen group to whom more is revealed than to others (4:11-12, 34), yet their general incomprehension up to 8:26 turns into a specific misunderstanding of the secret disclosed to them about a suffering Son of God. The secret is by no means perfectly kept (the demons in 1:24; 3:11, the sick in 10:47, and Jesus himself in 2:10, 19, 28; 9:2ff.; 11:1ff.; and 14:62 give it away). The early "secret epiphanies" or disclosures seem to lead up to Mark's special three epiphanies: the transfiguration (9:2-13), Jesus' self-identification before the high priest (14:61-62), and his appearance to the women culminating in his promise to meet his disciples and Peter in Galilee (16:7). The "secret" is a literary device used by Mark to withhold Jesus' identity until it is partially disclosed by the pagan centurion's exclamation of faith (15:39) and finally by the white-robed young man's, "He has been raised up. He is not here" (16:6; cf. 14:57-58).

4. For an exposition of their respective positions see Gerard S. Sloyan, "Recent Literature on the Trial Narratives of the Four Gospels," in *Critical History and Biblical Faith: New Testament Perspectives,* ed. Thomas J. Ryan, (Villanova, Pa.: Villanova University, 1979), 136–76. See also Vincent Taylor, *Mark.* Additional Note J, "The Construction of the Passion and Resurrection Narrative," 653–64, says that the evidence suggests that the Markan Passion narrative "came into existence in at least two main stages represented by A and B. A was non-Semitic and of a summary character . . . a simple straightforward narrative." B was strongly Semitic and "consisted of vivid self-contained narratives" (658). Taylor's scheme is as follows (sections containing possible Semitisms are underscored; probable later additions to A are in parentheses):

A. 14:1-2   14:10-11 (12-16), 17–21   14:26-31
B.   14:3-9   14:22-25   14:32-42

A. 14:43-46   (14:53)   14:55-64   15:1   15:3-5
B.   14:47-52   14:54   14:65, 66-72   15:2

A.   15:15   15:21-24   15:26   15:29-30
B. 15:6-14   15:16-20   15:25   15:27   15:31-32, 33

A. 15:34-37   15:39   15:42-6   (16:1-8)
B.   15:38   15:40-41   15:47

5. S. G. F. Brandon entitles chapter 5 of *Jesus and the Zealots* (Manchester: Manchester University Press, 1967) "The Markan Gospel: An *Apologia ad Christianos Romanos,*" 221–82; Raymond E. Brown cites the scholars who hold for a Roman origin of Mark, namely, Bernard Orchard, E. E. Ellis, Martin Hengel, Donald Senior, and C. C. Black; for

Galilee, Syria or Transjordan, H. C. Kee, Werner Kelber, Willi Marxsen, Burton Mack, Joel Marcus, and R. I. Rohrbaugh as the areas to which Mark was pertinent but concludes that "we cannot know precisely the locale addressed." See *An Introduction to the New Testament* (New York: Doubleday, 1997), 161–62; also Marie Noonan Sabin, *Reopening the Word: Reading Mark as Theology in the Context of Early Judaism* (New York: Oxford, 2002), on Mark as a basically midrashic writing.

6. Notably Theodore J. Weeden, *Mark* (Philadelphia: Fortress Press, 1971); Joseph Tyson, "The Blindness of the Disciples in Mark," *JBL* 80 (1961); Johannes Schreiber reported in Joachim Rohde, *Rediscovering the Teaching of the Evangelists* (Philadelphia: Westminster, 1969).

7. Norman Perrin, "Towards an Interpretation of the Gospel of Mark," in *Christology and a Modern Pilgrimage: A Discussion with Norman Perrin,* ed. Hans Dieter Betz (Missoula: Society of Biblical Literature, 1974).

8. For the existence of a pre-Markan cycle of such stories, see Leander E. Keck, "Mark 3:7-12 and Mark's Christology," *JBL* 84 (1965): 341–58; also Paul J. Achtemeier, "Toward the Isolation of Pre-Markan Miracle Catenae," *JBL* 89 (1970): 265–91; "The Origin and Function of Pre-Markan Miracle Catenae," *JBL* 91 (1972): 198–221. Achtemeier's two "chains" are Mark 4:35—6:44 and 6:45—8:26.

9. Perrin, "Towards an Interpretation," 55.

10. For the make up of the Sanhedrin before the fall of Jerusalem, see George Foot Moore, *Judaism in the First Centuries of the Christian Era* (Cambridge: Harvard University Press, 1927), 1:85, 260–62; on its Sadducean, that is, non-Pharisaic, character in Jesus' day, see Paul Winter, *On the Trial of Jesus,* Studia Judaica 1, 2d rev. ed. (Berlin: de Gruyter, 1974), 35–36.

11. Mark's narrative begins to become more cohesive in chapters 14–15 than it has been previously, although there are still clear traces of inserted elements (e.g., chaps. 12–13; 14:3-9). Moreover, Matthew does not feel free to depart from it much, esp. beginning with the arrest at Mark 14:43. Matthew does, however, have special material, such as the death of Judas, 27:3-10; Pilate washing his hands, 27:24-25; and the setting of the sepulcher guard, 27:62-66. Luke is also remarkably close to Mark's order and selection of incidents (adding only the formal charge before Pilate, 23:3; the hearing before Herod, 23:6-12; the road to Golgotha, 23:27-32; and the exchange between the two criminals on their crosses, 23:39-42). Even John, who has been entirely free in describing the earlier ministry, follows the Markan account or one very close to it. All this seems to indicate the existence of an authoritative, traditional source. Mark's modifications and additions to it can be explained in every case by some religious or apologetic concern. Other indications of the existence of such a source are a different chronology in 14:1-2 from Mark's own,

the source describing Jesus' arrest as occurring before the Passover while Mark makes it begin on Passover night, and a different ending to the source than the abrupt way in which Mark breaks off, an ending hinted at in 14:28 but fulfilled only in the brief phrase of 16:7b.

A theoretical reconstruction of the primitive Markan Passion source would be 14:1-2, 25-26, 43, 50-54, 65-72; 15:1-5, 15b, 21, 25-26, 34, 37. This spare total is arrived at by eliminating whatever elements could have been built up from Old Testament sources or as a result of apologetical considerations. In it, the Last Supper account, as we have it, is taken to have been built up on the basis of Jesus' vow of abstention from wine at a final meal (Mark 14:25; cf. Luke 22:14-18). Mark is not assumed to be the developer of all the narrative sections. Some could have existed in their developed form as part of the framework of tradition which came to him. Note the retention above in our list of the drafting of Simon of Cyrene (15:21), a detail that is self-authenticated as traditional because it is entirely without religious consequence. The above reconstruction follows Martin Dibelius, *From Tradition to Gospel*, trans. Bertram Lee Woolf (New York: Scribner's, 1935), and Bultmann, *Synoptic Tradition*. For a less radically critical view, see that of Vincent Taylor, n. 4 above. The flight from the garden of the naked young man (14:51-52), if a remembered detail, was probably made by Mark to be a type of the cowardly disciple of Mark's day rehabilitated through repentance clothed in a white garment (16:5).

12. For the view that the Passion story was the first part of the tradition to have been set in a continuous narrative, see Vincent Taylor, *The Formation of the Gospel Tradition*, 2d ed. (London: Macmillan, 1935), 44–62; and William R. Wilson, *The Execution of Jesus: A Judicial, Literary, and Historical Investigation* (New York: Scribner's, 1970), 29–30. For the case in favor of fragments of tradition and against the prevailing view of a unified, coherent, consecutive oral tradition, cf. Eta Linnemann, *Studien zur Passionsgeschichte* (Göttingen: Vandenhoeck & Ruprecht, 1970).

13. Cf. Pierre Benoit, "Le Mort de Judas," in *Exégèse et Théologie*, vol. 1 (Paris: Les Éditions du Cerf, 1961), 340–59; Bertil E. Gärtner, *Iscariot* (Philadelphia: Fortress Press, 1971).

14. Winter, *Trial*, 176.

15. Bultmann, *Synoptic Tradition*, 284; Winter, *Trial*, 68, 153–55; cf. Nils A. Dahl, "Der gekreuzigte Messias," in *Der historische Jesus und der kerygmatische Christus*, ed. H. Ristow and K. Matthiae, 2d ed. (Berlin: Evangelische Verlagsanstalt, 1961), 149–69.

16. See the two-volume work of Jean Juster, *Les Juifs dans l'Empire romain* (1914; repr. New York: B. Franklin, 1965); Hugo Mantel, *Studies in the History of the Sanhedrin* (Cambridge: Harvard University Press, 1965); J.

Blinzler, "The Jewish Punishment of Stoning in the New Testament Period," in *Judaism* 20 (1971): 147–61. Winter, *Trial*, 22–23, thinks that we do not have, even in the "First Mishnah," a record of the principles on which the Sadducee-dominated, first-century Sanhedrin operated. David Catchpole is of the opinion that no firm historical case can be made for illegalities in the Jewish "trial" as reported; *The Trial of Jesus: A Study in the Gospels and Jewish Historiography from 1770 to the Present Day*, Studia Post-Biblica 18 (Leiden: Brill, 1971), 256–60, 268–69.

17. For an exposition of Mark's use of interpolation which is described as a "major Marcan stylistic technique," see John R. Donahue, *Are You the Christ? The Trial Narrative in the Gospel of Mark* (Missoula, Mont.: Society of Biblical Literature, 1973), 77–84. The inserted portion serves to illuminate the interrupted material and vice versa. Donahue thinks that while vv. 53–65 derive from traditional materials, language and style show the passage to be a Markan composition. He hypothesizes that Mark chose a trial narrative as the setting for his main purpose, namely, to feature the christological titles of vv. 61-62, "Messiah," "son of the Blessed," and "Son of Man," but in the context of a trial or testing that would resonate with Mark's contemporaries as they underwent the trials in their locale that followed the destruction of Jerusalem and its Temple. He underscores the denial of the high priest that the three titles of the inserted material properly describe Jesus, while Peter's denial of him serves as the brackets of that narrative.

18. Thus, 3:22-30 (the Beelzebul charge) within 3:21 and 31-35 (Jesus' family think him beside himself); 5:25-34 (the woman with a flow of blood) between 5:21-24 and 35-43 (Jairus's daughter); 11:15-19 (temple cleansing) between 11:12-14 and 20-25 (fig tree cursed). The anointing at Bethany is placed between 14:1-2 and 14:10-11. The same seems clearly to be the case with the "night trial." Mark had the more extended tradition of an inquiry in religious circumstances (more extended, that is, than 15:1). He inserted this extended account within the story of Peter's denial (which occurs by firelight), probably for purposes of contrast, but also to fill up the time interval until morning. Verse 66 is an evident resumption of a narrative broken off after v. 54. See also n. 37, below, on Catchpole's use of "sandwich-structure" in Mark.

19. See Eduard Lohse, *History of the Suffering and Death of Jesus Christ* (Philadelphia: Fortress Press, 1967), 32–34, who sees a secondary meaning added to an original word of Jesus on the occasion of the temple cleansing.

20. See the discussion on 2 Corinthians 5:1 by W. D. Davies in *Paul and Rabbinic Judaism* (London: SPCK, 1948), 310–19; on Colossians 2:11, Eduard Lohse, *Colossians and Philemon,* Hermeneia (Philadelphia: Fortress Press, 1971), 102–3.

21. See C. H. Dodd, *According to the Scriptures: The Substructure of New Testament Theology* (London: Nisbet, 1952), 34–35, 121–22.

22. The discussion that follows is much indebted to Norman Perrin, *Rediscovering the Teaching of Jesus* (New York: Harper & Row, 1967), 164–81; he, in turn, depends for his interpretation of Mark 14:62 in part on Barnabas Lindars, *New Testament Apologetic: The Doctrinal Significance of the Old Testament Quotations* (Philadelphia: Westminster, 1961), 48–49.

23. Cf. J. Morgenstern, "The 'Son of Man' of Dan. 7:13f. A New Interpretation," *JBL* (1961): 65–77; cf. Douglas R. A. Hare's much more exhaustive research into the meaning of the term in Daniel and the various uses made of it by New Testament authors in *The Son of Man Tradition* (Minneapolis: Fortress Press, 1990), esp. Mark in 204–11, 277–80. His conclusion is that early Christian belief in the parousia, Jesus' coming in glory, had no need of Daniel 7:13 as its cornerstone but employed it and other OT texts merely to illustrate or flesh out that belief.

24. Cf. Matthew Black, "The Eschatology of the Similitudes of Enoch," *JTS* NS 3 (1952): 1–10. The translations given above follow that of R. H. Charles, in *The Apocrypha and Pseudepigrapha of the Old Testament* (Oxford: Clarendon, 1913), 2:235–37, except that in the famous passage at 71:14-16, where Charles changed the second person to the third, the text rather than his emendation has been followed. The possibility should be noted that the pertinent chapters of 1 Enoch may have been written after the New Testament, in which case Mark can contain nothing derived from them; cf. J. T. Milik, *Ten Years of Discovery in the Wilderness of Judaea*, trans. J. Strugnell, *SBT* 26 (1959), 33, where it is observed that nothing of 1 Enoch has been found at Qumrân. Milik, in light of further study of the Dead Sea Scrolls material, has, in more recent articles, stressed even more emphatically his opinion that the Enoch chapters are post–New Testament, likely from the second century CE; cf. "Problèmes de la littérature hénochique à la lumière des fragments araméens de Qumran," *HTR* 64 (1971): 333–78. E. Isaac comments favorably and unfavorably on Milik's dating in James A. Charlesworth, *The Old Testament Pseudepigrapha* (Garden City, N.Y.: Doubleday, 1983), 1:7, and cites a consensus of Pseudepigrapha scholars meeting in 1977 and 1978 that the similitudes (chaps. 37–71) are Jewish and date from the first century CE (7).

25. For the first two parables, see 38:1-6; 45:1-6.

26. Weeden, *Mark*, argues that *opsontai* cannot have an indefinite subject, let alone "men" or "the elect," since the Son of Man can appear only when world history is over; but "the curtain on the earthly plane of existence fell in 13:24a. . . . The arena of 13:24-26 is exclusively that of the cosmic-supernatural" (130).

Here, again, as with 1 Enoch, the date assigned to the Jewish apocalyptic document is important. Representative of those who think 4 Ezra
a pre-Christian book is Frederick Houk Borsch, *The Son of Man in Myth
and History* (Philadelphia: Westminster, 1967), 156–59. A significant
minority of scholars thinks it should be dated in the second century CE.

27. Weeden, *Mark*, 131.

28. Perrin, *Rediscovering*, 173–74, argues, nonetheless, for Mark 13:26
as a description of the parousia. His reasons are that (1) in no use made of
Daniel 7:13 outside the New Testament is the "clouds" phrase placed close
to the verb "coming," hence the change occurs "to make unambiguous the
fact that the clouds are the medium for the figure's movement and that the
movement is one from heaven to earth," and that (2) the Markan phrase "in
clouds," a change from Daniel's "on the clouds" (LXX or Theodotion's more
correct rendering of the Hebrew, "with clouds"), is a Christian *midrash
pesher* (that is, interpretative alteration) bringing the appearance of Jesus
into line with various Old Testament epiphanies where the phrase is used
(Exod. 16:10; 19:9; Lev. 16:2; Num. 11:25). While the second argument stri-
kes the present writer as persuasive, the first does not. If Mark is employing
v. 26 to describe the parousia (see the text preceding n. 24, 52, above), it is
in terms of a modification of Daniel 7:13 already in use in Christian circles
descriptive of his initial triumph over God's enemies in the glory of resur-
rection-ascension.

29. See Weeden, *Mark*, 135. He derives from Ferdinand Hahn, *Titles
of Jesus in Christology: Their History in Early Christianity* (London: Lut-
terworth; New York and Cleveland: World, 1969), 98, 125, arguments in
support of the position that Mark 14:61-62 is the "oldest statement we
have of the primitive community's belief in Jesus' future messiahship."

30. Perrin, *Rediscovering*, 175.

31. Bultmann, *Synoptic Tradition*, 270.

32. See Gustaf Dalman, *The Words of Jesus,* trans. D. M. Kay (Edinburgh: T. & T. Clark, 1902), 200.

33. Perrin connects this "you will see" and the "they will see" of 13:26
with the "they shall look on him whom they have thrust through" of
Zechariah 12:10 as part of a Passion apologetic tradition which preceded
the use of Daniel 7:13. See *Rediscovering*, 184–85.

34. S. G. F. Brandon holds in *Jesus and the Zealots: A Study of the
Political Factor in Primitive Christianity* (Manchester: Manchester University Press, 1967), that Jesus was delivered over to Rome by Jewish authorities for prosecution on a *civil* charge which was much later conceived to
be, in the Christian writings, the *religious* charge of blasphemy. Brandon
maintains that there was a gravitation of organized Zealotry toward the
person of Jesus in the 20s. There is no evidence for the existence of an

organized movement of that name until the 60s, making it hard to base the course of the infant church on events that had not yet occurred.

He sees Mark busy denigrating in particular the Twelve and the members of Jesus' family and assumes throughout the active interest of Jesus in violent revolt. Each time Jesus is described in the Gospels as discouraging the overtures of Zealot elements or sidestepping descriptions of himself as Messiah, Brandon sees deliberate alterations by a Markan hand.

35. On blasphemy, Leviticus 24:16 defines it as reviling God, that is, the divine Name; Mishnah "Sanhedrin" 7.5. E. P. Sanders in *Jewish Law from Jesus to the Mishnah; Five Studies* (Philadelphia: Trinity, 1990), 57–67, describes blasphemy as any utterance taken to threaten the divine unity or majesty. D. R. Catchpole, writing in E. Bammel, ed., *The Trial of Jesus,* "The Problem of the Historicity of the Sanhedrin Trial," SBT 2/13 (1970), 47–65, and in his *Trial . . . Historiography,* goes on the assumption that there was a full Sanhedrin hearing, a fact which, he thinks, Luke's source supports. His chief argument in favor of the dependability of Mark's account of the Sanhedrin trial is that "the 'sandwich-structure' is an interpretive device frequently used by Mark and has no bearing whatever on historicity" ("The Problem," 55). If Mark 14:65 is accepted as "a developed form of a tradition presented in a more primitive form in Luke 22:63-5," why discredit the historicity of vv. 55–64 which precede it? (ibid.) Catchpole cites all the historical reasons why a Sanhedrin trial was not inherently impossible. He is not much interested in the history of the Markan tradition in *Trial . . . Historiography* but does assume that it is not at odds with the historical source that underlies Luke.

36. Winter, "The Marcan Account of Jesus' Trial by the Sanhedrin" *JTS* NS 14 (1963), 102: "The pericope of the Sanhedrin's night session has been superimposed on material . . . collected from earlier tradition of Jesus' arrest with [the Evangelist's] own interpretation. It follows that no historical deductions can be made from an inserted passage which is in discord with the primary account of Jesus' arrest and trial and the grounds on which he was sentenced to death."

37. Catchpole, *Trial . . . Historiography* 125, 130; on the latter page we read, at the conclusion of arguments de-emphasizing the teaching of Jesus as the cause of opposition by Jewish groups: "The grounds for his condemnation were of a political character."

38. Bultmann, *Synoptic Tradition,* 271 (supplemental material). Taylor, *Mark,* 570–71, agrees. That the "some" in Mark 14:65 are Sanhedrin members is improbable; they are probably the men guarding Jesus, as in Luke 22:64.

39. Bultmann, *Synoptic Tradition,* 276 (supplemental material).

40. Ibid., 277.

41. Winter, *Trial,* 21.

42. Catchpole, "The Problem," in *Trial . . . Historiography,* 55.

43. Alfred Loisy, *The Origins of the New Testament* (New York: Collier, 1962), 120.

44. Ched Myers, *Binding the Strong Man. A Political Reading of Mark's Story of Jesus* (Maryknoll, N.Y.: Orbis Books, 1997), 377.

45. Ibid. 377.

46. Bultmann, *Synoptic Tradition*, 269.

47. T. Alec Burkill, *Mysterious Revelation: An Examination of the Philosophy of St. Mark's Gospel*, (Cornell: Cornell University Press), 243–44. He also observes the contrast between the courage of Jesus and the cowardice of Peter, 14:53-55; between the innocent Jesus and the guilty Barabbas, 15:6-8; and between "The King of the Jews" and the two convicted criminals, 15:26-27.

48. Thus, the practice of *lectisternium* or loosening of the chains of prisoners on feasts of the gods attested to by Livy; this, however, was a scheme of mass pardons; cf. J. Merkel, "Die Begnadigung am Passahfeste," *ZNW* 6 (1905): 293–316; cf. also the reference cited by Adolf Deissmann, *Light from the Ancient East,* 2d ed. (London: Hodder & Stoughton, 1927), 269, in which G. Septimius Vegetus says to an Egyptian named Phibion: "You were worthy of scourging . . . but I give you to the people."

49. Bultmann, *Synoptic Tradition*, 279.

50. Annie Jaubert is the best-known modern proponent of the view that Jesus and his friends followed an older, priestly mode of reckoning, probably the solar calendar known from the book of Jubilees. She has plotted all the happenings of the last week of Jesus' life in terms of such a calendar, beginning with the supper and his subsequent arrest on Tuesday night. See *The Date of the Last Supper* (Staten Island, N.Y.: Alba House, 1965). The same author has also written on this question in *RB* 65 (1968): 214–48; and *NTS* 7 (1960–61): 1–30; 14 (1967–68): 145–47; cf. also Eugen Ruckstuhl, *Chronology of the Last Days of Jesus: A Critical Study* (New York: Desclée, 1965).

51. The sole information on the high priests in office during Jesus' lifetime is from Josephus's *Antiquities of the Jews.* Ananus or Hanan (the Annas of the Gospels) served from 6 CE to 15 CE under Valerius Gratus, after Quirinius, the legate of Syria, deposed Joazar—against whom the people had revolted. There were probably three others before Caiaphas, the second of them Eleazar, son of Annas, between 15 and 26, when Pilate took office. Cf. *Ant.* 18. 26. 34, 35, 95 (18.2.1; 2.2; 4.3). Also E. M. Smallwood, "High Priests and Politics in Roman Palestine," *JTS* NS 13 (1962): 14–34.

CHAPTER 4—The HISTORY of the TRADITION of the INTERROGATION and TRIAL in MATTHEW

1. Gerhard Barth, "Matthew's Understanding of the Law," in *Tradition and Interpretation in Matthew*, ed. G. Bornkamm, G. Barth, and H. J. Held, trans. Percy Scott (Philadelphia: Westminster, 1963), 146. For a careful analysis of the direct dependencies of Matthew on Mark, the minor agreements of Matthew and Luke against Mark, and the special agreements of Matthew and John, see Nils A. Dahl, "Die Passionsgeschichte bei Matthäus," *NTS* 2 (1955–56): 17–32, and in much greater detail Donald P. Senior, *The Passion Narrative according to Matthew: A Redactional Study* (Leuven: Leuven University Press, 1975). For a succinct but dependable commentary on the Passion narrative see Benedict T. Viviano, "The Gospel according to Matthew," in Raymond E. Brown, Joseph A. Fitzmyer, and Roland E. Murphy, eds., *The New Jerome Biblical Commentary* (Englewood Cliffs, N.J.: Prentice Hall, 1990), 146–65, 669–73.

2. See *The Babylonian Talmud*, ed. Isidore Epstein, *Seder Nezikin V, Sanhedrin*, vol. 1 (London: Soncino, 1935), *Yoma* 39*b*, 185–88; Jerusalem Talmud, *Yoma* 43*c*; cf. also *Kommentar zum Neuen Testament aus Talmud und Midrasch*, ed. H. L. Strack and P. Billerbeck (Munich: Beck, 1922), vol. 1, 1003–4, 1045. In Josephus, *Jewish War* 6.301–09 (6.5.3), a certain Jesus the son of Ananus proclaimed the destruction of the temple loudly before it came down. Lloyd Gaston's *No Stone on Another: Studies in the Significance of the Fall of Jerusalem in the Synoptic Gospels* (Leiden: Brill, 1970), holds that "the new temple was not an important part of Jewish eschatology before 70 CE, and the Messiah was never expected to build it anyway" (105). Gaston concedes that the Targum to Zechariah 6:12-13 identifies the Messiah as a Temple builder but says that this is a much later development (149). Before the year 70, the restoration of Jerusalem-Zion was the theme in possession, with no special attention paid to the Messiah as the restorer of public worship. He concludes that Mark in the first half of 14:58 has attributed a saying of Stephen about the destruction to Jesus (242).

3. See M. Jack Suggs, *Wisdom, Christology, and Law in Matthew's Gospel* (Cambridge: Harvard University Press, 1970), 63–71.

4. Rudolf Bultmann, *The History of the Synoptic Tradition* (German, 1921), Eng. trans. by John Marsh. 2d ed. (New York: Harper & Row; Oxford: Basil Blackwell, 1968), 121.

5. Thus J. Schneider, *"exorkizō,"* in *TDNT* 5: 465.

6. It is usual to argue that the tendency of the Evangelists to blame the Sanhedrin for Jesus' death increases from Mark, through Matthew and Luke, to John. David R. Catchpole, *The Trial of Jesus: A Study in the Gospels*

and Jewish Historiography from 1770 to the Present Day, Studia Post-Biblica 18 (Leiden: Brill, 1971), finds rather that the sequence is "from plain Sanhedrin proceedings (Mark and Matthew) to much less plain ones (Luke) and finally to no trial at all in John (at least in chap. 18)!"

7. Theodore J. Weeden, *Mark* (Philadelphia: Fortress Press, 1971), 23–26.

8. Krister Stendahl deals at length with this intricate targumic product in *The School of St. Matthew and Its Use of the Old Testament* (Philadelphia: Fortress Press, 1968; first published 1954), 120–26. Robert Horton Gundry holds, against Stendahl, that no special Matthean school practicing *pesher* (explanation)-type exegesis is necessary to account for the formula quotations in that Gospel, but that the trilingual milieu of New Testament times resulted in the ordinary citation technique of the Synoptics, of which Matthew is simply a part. The real exception is Mark, who, like the other New Testament writers, adheres to the LXX. Cf. Gundry's *The Use of the Old Testament in St. Matthew's Gospel* (Leiden: Brill, 1967).

9. Stendahl, *The School of St. Matthew,* 123; for Gundry, it is "because the manifestness of the quotation from Zech and the lack of verbal resemblance to Jer would cause the Jer-side . . . to be lost" (125).

10. Cf. Krister Stendahl, "Matthew," in *Peake's Commentary on the Bible,* eds. Matthew Black and Harold H. Rowley, (London: Nelson, 1962), 796 (sec. 694b).

11. For Gundry's discussion of this text, see his *Use of the Old Testament,* 122–27: "Mt sees parallels between the guilt of Judah and Jerusalem in shedding innocent blood and that of Judas . . . between the two occurrences of *yōtsēr* in Jer. 19:1, 11 . . . and the circumstance that the chief priests bought the field *of a potter,* between the prominence of 'the elders' and 'the (chief) priests' in both passages, between the burial of the Judaeans in the Valley of Hinnom and the burial of Judas in the potter's field . . ." (125).

12. C. S. C. Williams, "The Synoptic Problem," in *Peake's Commentary,* 753–54.

13. Stendahl, "Matthew," 769.

14. Ibid., 770.

15. Barth, "Matthew's Understanding of the Law," 146.

16. Gaston, *No Stone on Another,* 486.

17. Ibid., 487.

CHAPTER 5—The INQUEST and TRIAL NARRATIVES in the GOSPEL according to LUKE

1. Vincent Taylor, *The Passion Narrative of St. Luke: A Critical and Historical Investigation,* ed. O. E. Evans (Cambridge: Cambridge University

Press, 1972), 50. For a recent, exhaustive inquiry into a particular aspect of Luke's Passion account see Jay M. Harrington, *The Lukan Passion Narrative: The Markan Material in Luke 22:54—23:35* (Leiden: Brill, 2000), 364–496, 710–804. See also Luke Timothy Johnson, *The Gospel of Luke*, "Sacra Pagina" (Collegeville, Minn.: Liturgical Press, 1991), 356–75.

2. Luke 22:19b-20 is "read by p[75], all Greek uncial manuscript except D, all the Versions except a few manuscript of the Old Latin and sy[s] and sy[c], Marcion, Justin, and probably Tatian" (Taylor, *Passion Narrative*, 50). Two Old Latin manuscript read 15, 16, 19a, 17, 18, an order that occurs with minor variations in the Old Syriac. The two verses are probably drawn form a liturgical source which also provided Paul with 1 Corinthians 11:23-25 (so Schürmann, Taylor, and Jeremias). Long disputed as genuine because thought to be an interpolation from 1 Corinthians 11, these verses have now come to be accepted quite widely. (Cf. Taylor, *Passion Narrative*, 51.)

There are many non-Pauline features in 1 Corinthians 11:23-25, leading Schürmann in his careful analysis to suppose that Paul is editing a liturgical source. See Heinz Schürmann, *A Source-Critical Exegesis of the Lukan Last Supper Account xxii.7—38: II. The Consecratory Formula Lk 22, 19—20* (in German; Münster: Aschendorff, 1955). The Lord's Supper narrative in Luke, Schürmann says, has idioms foreign to Paul. He is of the opinion that Luke in 22:19-20 is dependent, not on Paul, but on the same liturgical source, and that it is Luke who gives the original text rather than Paul in four out of the five cases that he selects for special examination. All of this work is done by comparing the words and phrases of the two New Testament writers with their normal usage. Thus, Luke 22:19-20 is shown to contain no characteristic Lukan words. The pre-Lukan liturgical source of vv. 19 and 20 (and 19a may come from Mark, since Luke seems prone to use opening words in parallel Markan narratives) is thought to have come from Antioch some time between the years 30 and 40. Schürmann's reconstruction of this original account of the Eucharist is as follows: "And taking bread, he offered a blessing in thanks, broke it and gave it to them, and said: '(Take this[?]) This is my body which is given for you. Do this as a memorial (remembrance) of me.' He did the same with the cup after eating, saying: 'This cup is the new covenant in my blood.'"

Part of the reason why vv. 19b-20 were thought non-genuine was the supposition that later copyists, nervous over the sequence cup-bread in vv. 17-19a, inserted the verse and a half to supply the more familiar bread-cup sequence. But Luke could easily have done this from a liturgy on his own, having first provided the eschatological development he was more interested in.

3. Taylor, *Passion Narrative*, 59, 61.

4. Ibid., 66.

5. Ibid., 67.

6. REB and NAB (1970) render the "It is enough" or "Enough!" in everyday speech of 22:38 as a cutting off of the conversation by Jesus, as in the LXX of Deuteronomy 3:26. It is unthinkable that "It is enough" is meant to be Jesus' comment on the sufficiency of swords for a Zealot uprising. See David R. Catchpole, *The Trial of Jesus: A Study in the Gospels and Jewish Historiography from 1770 to the Present Day,* Studia Post-Biblica 18 (Leiden: Brill, 1971), 124–25, for a discussion of the translation possibilities.

7. David Flusser, in general support of R. L. Lindsey's theory that Luke *preceded* Mark in composition (Robert Lisle Lindsey, *A Hebrew Translation of the Gospel of Mark* [Jerusalem: Dugith, Baptist House, 1969]), writes in a foreword that Luke never mentions Jesus' condemnation by the Jewish authorities as Mark does (10:33-34, contrast Luke 18:31-32), nor does he speak of blasphemy or the tearing of the high priest's clothes (Mark 14:63-64, contrast Luke 22:70-71). Flusser concludes that "Luke has not been influenced by the redactic operation of our Mark" (7) and that, while Luke "does not hesitate to report the delivery of Jesus to Pilate by Jewish authorities" (5), he is working from materials that precede Mark's dramatized attempt at popularization. Flusser repeats these views in his article "A Literary Approach to the Trial of Jesus" in the symposium in *Judaism* 20 (1971): 32–36.

8. Paul Feine was the first to describe Luke's use of a third source besides Mark and Q, usually denoted S on the continent and L by British and North American scholars (Gotha, 1891). Taylor had previously argued for the "proto-Luke hypothesis" in his thesis, *Behind the Third Gospel* (Oxford: Clarendon, 1926). He regards Mark as Luke's main source and devotes his study to showing how he used it. But he stops his detailed investigation at Luke 22:13, holding that from v. 14 onward Luke depends on a special written source to which he adds extracts from Mark. See now his posthumous *Passion Narrative.* Gerhard Schneider maintains that in his account of the denial, the mocking, and the hearing before the priests Luke followed a non-Markan Passion source that spoke of arrest, mockery, and morning trial, into which he introduced, from Mark, the story of Peter's denial *Verleugnung, Verspottung und Verhör Jesu nach Lukas 22, 54-71,* Studien zum Alten und Neuen Testament 22 (Munich: Kosel Verlag, 1969).

For the sake of completeness, it should be worthwhile merely to indicate Taylor's conclusions regarding the remainder of the Passion material in Luke. The journey to the cross (23:26-32) is non-Markan except for the first verse, which derives from Mark 15:21, the drafting of Simon of Cyrene. Into a non-Markan source on the crucifixion narrative (23:33-49) the following insertions have been made from Mark: vv. 34*b*, 38, 44-45, and 49. Mark is Luke's source for the burial narrative (23:50-54) "without any clear sign of a second source except a knowledge of Johannine tradition" (*Passion Narrative*, 101). At the conclusion, Taylor supplies in English the text of the source that his study has prepared us for, complete with insertions from Mark and omissions according to Luke's usage (127–32). The action of the women (23:55-56*a*) is on all accounts non-Markan, as is the visit to the tomb (23:56*b*—24:11), with the possible exception of Markan insertions at 24:1-3 and 10*a*; this, against the position that the pericope is an edited version of Mark 16:1-8. Verse 12 shows an acquaintance with the tradition about Peter and the wrappings in John 20:3-7. The story of the journey to Emmaus is told only by Luke (24:13-35) and seems to be Luke's embellishment of an existing tradition, possibly the expanding of an earlier source. The account of the appearance to the eleven (24:36-49) is in the latter category, while the concluding summary on the ascension (vv. 50-53) is Luke's composition. If Luke is adapting an earlier source, this is hidden by his use of many words and phrases peculiar to him, a vocabulary like that with which he will open his book of Acts.

9. In addition to vol. 2 cited in n. 2 above: vol. 1, *Der Paschamahlbericht, Lk 22 (7-14), 15-18* (1953) and vol. 3, *Jesu Abschiedsrede, Lk 22, 21-38* (1957).

10. F. Rehkopf, *Die lukanische Sonderquelle, ihr Umfang und Sprachgebrauch* (Tübingen: Mohr, 1959).

11. Burton Scott Easton, *The Gospel according to Luke* (New York: Scribner's, 1926).

12. S. G. F. Brandon, *Jesus and the Zealots: A Study of the Political Factor in Primitive Christianity* (Manchester: Manchester University Press, 1967), 340–41; Catchpole, in *Trial . . . Historiography*, 118–26, engages in a full-scale refutation of Brandon's theory that Jesus was Zealot-like and that Mark created the image of a "pacific Christ."

13. Catchpole, *Trial . . . Historiography*, 198–200.

14. H. E. Tödt, *The Son of Man in the Synoptic Tradition,* trans. Dorothea M. Barton (Philadelphia: Westminster, 1965), 102.

15. Catchpole, *Trial . . . Historiography*, 200. He finds Tödt, Conzelmann, and Flender at fault in attributing these verses to Lukan theology.

16. Tödt, *Son of Man*, 83. Cf. Hans Conzelmann, *The Theology of St. Luke,* trans. G. Buswell (New York: Harper & Row, 1961), 84, n. 3.

17. Cf. Helmut Flender, *St. Luke: Theologian of Redemptive History,* trans. Reginald H. and Ilse Fuller (Philadelphia: Fortress Press, 1967), 101.

18. Ibid., 45.

19. Cf. Catchpole, *Trial . . . Historiography*, 201.

20. Catchpole argues carefully and at length against Winter's contention that Luke's source (L) was relatively brief and that it departed notably from the traditions on which Mark based himself. Cf. ibid., 208–20.

CHAPTER 6—The CAIAPHAS and PILATE NARRATIVES in JOHN

1. Rudolf Bultmann, *Das Evangelium des Johannes,* Meyers Kritisch–Exegetischer Kommentar (Göttingen: Vandenhoeck & Ruprecht, 1941). A study of some of the problems Bultmann raised was done by Eugen Ruckstuhl, *Die literarische Einheit des Johannesevangeliums: Der gegenwärtige Stand der einschlägigen Forschung,* Studia Friburgensia n.s. 3 (Freiburg: Herder, 1951). His later *Chronology of the Last Days of Jesus* (New York: Desclée, 1965) attempts to prove Jaubert wrong in her Tuesday night "Date de la Cène."

2. D. Moody Smith, *The Composition and Order of the Fourth Gospel: Bultmann's Literary Theory* (New Haven: Yale University Press, 1965).

3. Robert Tomson Fortna, *The Gospel of Signs: A Reconstruction of the Narrative Source Underlying the Fourth Gospel,* SNTSMS 11 (1970). Fortna's reconstruction appears in Greek (Nestle's 25th edition) on 235–45. He followed it with the highly nuanced *The Fourth Gospel and Its Predecessor* (Philadelphia: Fortress Press, 1988). For recent scholarship on this Gospel, see Gerard S. Sloyan, *What Are They Saying about John?* 2d. rev. ed., (Mahwah, N.J.: Paulist, 2006).

4. Ivor Buse, "St. John and the Marcan Passion Narrative, *NTS* 4 (1957–58): 215–19. For a summary of theories on the Johannine trial accounts, cf. Ferdinand Hahn, "Der Prozess Jesu nach den Johannesevangelium: Eine redaktionsgeschichtliche Untersuchung," in *Evangelisch-Katholischer Kommentar zum Neuen Testament, Vorarbeiten Heft 2* (Zürich–Einsiedeln: Benziger; Neukirchen–Vluyn: Neukirchener Verlag, 1970), 23–96.

5. Peder Borgen, "John and the Synoptics in the Passion Narrative," *NTS* 5 (1958–59): 246–59; cf. D. Moody Smith, *John among the Gospels,* 2d rev. ed. (Minneapolis: Fortress Press, 1992), 141–58, esp. for recent theories of John's relation to Mark and/or Markan sources.

6. Smith, *John among the Gospels,* 254–55.

7. Ibid., 255–56.

8. Ivor Buse, "St. John and the Passion Narratives of St. Matthew and St. Luke," *NTS* 7 (1960–61): 65–76, esp. 68.

9. Ibid., 75.

10. Fortna, *Gospel of Signs,* 114, n. 10; the material that follows in the text above is a summary of Fortna's *SQ.*

11. For this terminology as descriptive of Jewish soldiery, cf. Judith 14:12, 2 Maccabees 8:22; 12:20, 22; Josephus, *Ant.* 17.215 (17.9.3); *Jewish War* 2.578 (2.20.7); discussion in David R. Catchpole, *The Trial of Jesus: A Study in the Gospels and Jewish Historiography from 1770 to the Present Day,* Studia Post-Biblica 18 (Leiden: Brill, 1971), 148–50; Josef Blinzler, *The Trial of Jesus: The Jewish and Roman Proceedings against Jesus Christ Described and Assessed from the Oldest Accounts,* trans. I. and F. McHugh (Westminster, Md.: Newman, 1959), 66–70.

12. Fortna, *Gospel of Signs,* 230, cf. 32.

13. Thus C. H. Dodd, *Historical Tradition in the Fourth Gospel* (New York: Cambridge University Press, 1963), 76–77, who says that a book of testimonies portraying Jesus as the Righteous Sufferer may underlie what is otherwise based on historical tradition in this account.

14. John's phrase to describe Caiaphas at 18:13, "who was high priest in (lit. of) that year," is a repetition of his own usage in 11:49; also 51, where the participle is used rather than the imperfect "was." Bultmann finds John simply in error in his supposition that Jewish high priests were changed yearly like pagan priests in Asia Minor, (Rudolf Bultmann, *The History of the Synoptic Tradition* [German, 1921], Eng. trans. by John Marsh. 2d ed. [New York: Harper & Row; Oxford: Basil Blackwell, 1968], 410, n. 10). Raymond E. Brown is inclined by the participial phrase to see John's emphasis on *that* year, in a use the equivalent of the temporal genitive (*The Gospel according to John [1–12],* Anchor Bible 29 [Garden City, N.Y.: Doubleday, 1966], 440). He cites Blass-Debrunner, *A Greek Grammar of the New Testament and Other Early Christian Literature,* trans. R. Funk (Chicago: University of Chicago Press, 1961), sec. 186(2), where it is allowed, but as doubtful, a fact that Bultmann uses against the Johannine use as a genitive of time.

15. Luke is an exception by letting Peter's denials take up the night, with no trial until morning.

16. Cf. Fortna, *Gospel of Signs,* 118.

17. In v. 31*a* Pilate offers Jesus to the *Ioudaîoi* to pass judgment on him according to their Law. He will do something similar when he proposes, with total historical improbability but probable sarcasm at their power-lessness, that they crucify him themselves (19:6). They respond in the first instance, "We may not put anyone to death" (18:31*b*). This statement has been much argued in terms of its historical accuracy, namely, whether the Jewish people had retained the right under the Romans to execute capital sentence for offenses against Mosaic Law. (For a discussion of the question, see Jean Juster, *Les Juifs dans l'Empire romain* [1914; repr. New York: B. Franklin, 1965], who reversed two hundred years of Jewish argumentation by maintaining that the Sanhedrin had authority to have Jesus

executed by stoning, hence that John is wrong. Goguel, Lietzmann, Bur-kill, and Winter follow him in this; Blinzler, Benoit, and Jeremias do not. Catchpole presents the arguments of Juster and all who follow him, *Trial . . . Historiography*, 236–60; also the argument of R. W. Husband, *The Prosecution of Jesus* (Princeton: Princeton University Press, 1916), who theorized that there was a preliminary Jewish hearing before a Roman trial. John may conceivably be reflecting an accurate historical remembrance; this is doubtful, but the argument continues. That is not, however, why John makes the statement. He is talking about the fulfillment of prophecy (v. 32), much like 12:33; cf. also 18:9. If Jesus were to die by any way but crucifixion—the way John knows he did die—then his death by "being raised up" (see the serpent image, 3:14*b*; cf. 8:28*a*; 12:32) would not have been realized. The statement of 18:31*b* is therefore meant to be neither historical nor absolute but a condition that must be met if prophecy is to be fulfilled—the elevated Jesus as a saving sign. But, for John, prophecy had to be fulfilled. That is the point of the remark that he attributed to the crowd: *they* could not put Jesus to death; there had to be a Roman crucifixion because when he wrote there had been one.

18. Dodd, *Historical Tradition*, 83.

19. For the identity of "the Jews," most often but not always a term of hostility in the fourth Gospel, see the opinions of François Vouga, *Le Cadre historique et l'intention théologique de Jean* (Paris, Beauchesne, 1977), and John Ashton, *Understanding the Fourth Gospel* (Oxford: Clarendon, 1991), summarized along with others in Gerard S. Sloyan, *What Are They Saying About John?* In John, where everyone is ethnically Jewish other than a sprinkling of Samaritans and the occupying army, the *Ioudaioi* are usually to be identified with the Temple priesthood and the elders; sometimes also with the Pharisees, overzealous for the Law, in which case Pharisees and Jews are interchangeable terms. They are used by John as a cipher for those elements among the Jewish people who are harassing the Johannine church, also ethnically Jewish.

CHAPTER 7—CONCLUSIONS

1. The first appearance of the ugly term "Christ-killers" (*Christok-tonōn*) occurs in John Chrysostom, *Against the Jews*, Homily 1.4 (PG 48.862); in Latin the term *deicide*, because of belief in the divinity of Christ, came to be used. The total falsehood of the charge is featured in *Nostra Aetate* 4 of Vatican II, but without the use of either term.

2. David Flusser, "A Literary Approach to the Trial of Jesus," *Judaism* 20 (1971): 33. A similar view is that of Franz E. Meyer, who distinguishes

between the actual Sanhedrin (Beth Din ha-Gadol) and "their Sanhedrin" of Luke 22:66, a privy council made up of Sadducees which delivered Jesus over to Pilate; see "Einige Bemerkungen zur Bedeutung des Terminus 'Synhedrion' in den Schriften des Neuen Testament," *NTS* 14 (1967–68): 545–51.

3. See above, pp. 72, 74–75.

4. Helpful in this connection might be the present writer's *The Crucifixion of Jesus: History, Myth, Faith* (Minneapolis: Fortress Press, 1995), which devotes one chapter to this mode of execution, another to the charge by the church fathers that the Jews of Jerusalem were responsible for Jesus' death, and a third to the development of the Christian doctrine of human redemption. The remainder of the book traces the wide expression of what might be called Calvary piety in the Christian West, Catholic and Protestant, but not the Orthodox East, except for one aspect of Russian piety.

⊕ ⊕ ⊕ ⊕ ⊕ ⊕

SELECT BIBLIOGRAPHY
on the PASSION and TRIAL of JESUS

Ashton, John. "Passion and Resurrection." In *Understanding the Fourth Gospel*. Oxford: Clarendon, 1991, 485–514. See also Ashton's important discussion of the likelihood that "the Jews" did not mean Judaeans, but was a self-denomination of Torah-zealous returnees from exile, not one devised by John, 152–59.

Bammel, Ernst, ed. *The Trial of Jesus: Cambridge Studies in Honour of C. F. D. Moule. SBT* 2/13 (1970). Among the contributors, besides the editor, are Peter Richardson, Margaret Baker, H. Merkel, J. E. Allen, H. W. Hoehner, J. Pobee, and G. MacRae. For Blinzler, Catchpole, Horbury, and O'Neill, see below.

Benoit, Pierre, O.P. *Jesus and the Gospel*. Vol. 1. London: Darton, Longman & Todd, 1973, 123–208. Scholarly articles and reviews, 1940–54, reprinted in Benoit's *Exégèse et Théologie* (1961), on the trial, passion sites, and Judas.

———. *The Passion and Resurrection of Jesus Christ*. New York: Herder & Herder; London: Darton, Longman & Todd, 1969.

Best, Ernest. *The Temptation and the Passion: The Markan Soteriology. SNTSMS* 2 (1965).

Black, Matthew. "The Arrest and Trial of Jesus and the Date of the Last Supper." In *New Testament Essays: Studies in Memory of Thomas Walter Manson, 1893-1958*. Ed. A. J. B. Higgins. Manchester: Manchester University Press, 1959, 19-33.

———. "The 'Son of Man' Passion Sayings in the Gospel Tradition." *ZNW* 60 (1969): 1-8. *NT Abstracts* 14 (1969): 425.

Blinzler, Josef. *The Trial of Jesus: The Jewish and Roman Proceedings against Jesus Christ Described and Assessed from the Oldest Accounts*. Westminster, Md.: Newman Press, 1959.

———. "The Trial of Jesus in the Light of History." *Judaism* 20 (1971): 49-55.

Borgen, Peder. "John and the Synoptics in the Passion Narrative." *NTS* 5 (1958-59): 246-59.

Bornhäuser, Karl. *The Death and Resurrection of Christ*. London: Independent Press, 1958.

Brandon, S. G. F. *Jesus and the Zealots: A Study of the Political Factor in Primitive Christianity*. Manchester: Manchester University Press, 1967.

———. *The Trial of Jesus of Nazareth*. New York: Stein & Day; London: B. T. Batsford, 1968.

Brown, Raymond E. *The Death of the Messiah: From Gethsemane to the Grave: A Commentary on the Passion Narratives*. 2 vols. New York: Doubleday, 1994.

Bultmann, Rudolf. *The History of the Synoptic Tradition*. New York: Harper & Row, 1968 (1921). See the analysis of individual sections of the passion, 262-74, and "The History of the Tradition of the Passion," 275-84.

Carter, Warren. *Pontius Pilate: Roman Governor*. Collegeville, Minn.: Liturgical Press, 2003.

Catchpole, David R. "The Answer of Jesus to Caiaphas (Matt. xxvi. 64)." *NTS* 17 (1970-71): 213-26. *NT Abstracts* 15: 862.

———. "The Problem of the Hitoricity of the Sanhedrin," in Bammel above.

———. *The Trial of Jesus: A Study in the Gospels and Jewish Historiography from 1770 to the Present Day*. Leiden: Brill, 1971.

Cohn, Haim H. "Reflections on the Trial of Jesus." *Judaism* 20 (1971): 10-23. *NT Abstracts* 15: 811.

———. *The Trial and Death of Jesus*. New York: Harper & Row, 1971; London: Weidenfeld & Nicholson, 1972.

Connolly-Weinert, Frank. "Assessing Omissions as Redaction: Luke's Handling of the Charge against Jesus as Detractor of the Temple." In *To Touch the Text: Studies in Honor Joseph A Fitzmyer, S.J.* Ed. M. P. Horgan and P. J. Kobelski. New York: Crossroad, 1989, 358-68.

Conzelmann, Hans. "History and Theology in the Passion Narratives of the Synoptic Gospels." *Interpretation* 24 (1970): 178–97. *NT Abstracts* 15 (1970): 117. Cf. also Haenchen below and Viering, Fritz, ed. *Zur Bedeutung des Todes Jesu*. Gütersloh: Mohn, 1967.

Cullmann, Oscar. *The State in the New Testament*. New York: Scribner's, 1966.

Dodd, C. H. "The Historical Problem of the Death of Jesus." In *More New Testament Studies*. Grand Rapids: Eerdmans, 1968: 84–101.

Donahue, John R. *Are You the Christ? The Trial Narrative in the Gospel of Mark*. Missoula, Mont.: Society of Biblical Literature, 1973.

Enslin, Morton S. "The Temple and the Cross." *Judaism* 20 (1971): 24–31. *NT Abstracts* 15 (1971): 812.

Finegan, Jack. *Die Überlieferung der Leidens- und Auferstehungsgeschichte Jesu*. Beihefte zur *ZNW* 15 (1934). An older but still basic form-critical analysis.

Fitzmyer, Joseph A. "Anti-Semitism and the Cry of 'All the People' (Mt. 27:25)." *Theological Studies* 26 (1965): 667–71.

Flusser, David. "A Literary Approach to the Trial of Jesus." *Judaism* 20 (1971): 32–36. See below, 137, n. 2; also chap. 7, n. 2, and chap. 5, n. 7. *NT Abstracts* 15 (1970): 813. Flusser, Professor of Comparative Religion at Hebrew University, Jerusalem, has also written a "life," *Jesus* (New York: Herder & Herder, 1969).

Gordis, Robert, ed. "The Trial of Jesus in the Light of History: A Symposium." *Judaism* 20 (1971): 6–74. See above, chap. 1, n. 1.

Grant, Robert M. "The Trial of Jesus in the Light of History." *Judaism* 20 (1971): 37–42. See above, chap. 1, n. 2. *NT Abstracts* 15 (1971): 814.

Gundry, Robert H. *Mark: A Commentary on His Apology for the Cross*. Grand Rapids: Eerdmans, 1993.

Haenchen, Ernst. "History and Interpretation in the Johannine Passion Narrative." *Interpretation* 24 (1970): 198–219. *NT Abstracts* 15 (1970): 210.

Hare, Douglas R. A. *The Theme of Jewish Persecution of Christians in the Gospel according to St. Matthew*. Cambridge, U.P. 1969.

Harrington, Jay M. *The Lukan Passion Narrative: The Markan Material in Luke 22:54—23:25*. Leiden: Brill, 2000.

———. *The Son of Man Tradition*. Minneapolis, Fortress Press, 1990.

Horbury, William. "The Passion Narratives and Historical Criticism." *Theology* 75 (1972): 58–71. *NT Abstracts* 16 (1972): 811.

———. "The Trial of Jesus in Jewish Tradition." In Bammel, ed., *Trial* (Moule Festschrift; cited in Bammel above), 103–21. Especially examines a Cambridge fragment from the Cairo Geniza of the "Toledoth Yeshu."

Horvath, T. "Why Was Jesus Brought to Pilate?" *NovT* 11 (1969): 174–84. *NT Abstracts* 14 (1969): 440.

Husband, Richard Wellington. "The Pardoning of Prisoners by Pilate." *American Journal of Theology* 21 (1917): 110–16.

———. *The Prosecution of Jesus: Its Date, History and Legality.* Princeton: Princeton University Press, 1916. See above, chap. 6, n. 17. He concluded that the Sanhedrin hearing was a "grand jury" action, not a trial, to gather evidence for an indictment to present to Pilate, who conducted the only trial of Jesus.

Isaac, Jules. *Jesus and Israel.* New York: Holt, Rinehart & Winston, 1971.

Jaubert, Annie. *The Date of the Last Supper.* Staten Island, N.Y.: Alba House, 1965.

Kilpatrick, G. D. *The Trial of Jesus.* 1952. New York: Oxford University Press, 1953. While recognizing some truth in Lietzmann's view on the trial, this lecture contends that Mark 14: 55-65 "need not be a fiction of the Early Church" (p. 20); there was a Jewish hearing, where a statement of Jesus about destroying the temple, more akin to Matthew 26:60-61 than to Mark 14:56-59, was rejected as blasphemous and where the high priest probably asked Jesus about his claim to be king of Israel as well as Messiah—Son of God; and the Sanhedrin could not itself at this period inflict the death penalty (as John 18:31 correctly states).

Kosmala, Hans. "'His Blood on Us and Our Children' (The Background of Mat. 27, 24–25)." *Annual of the Swedish Theological Institute* (Jerusalem) 7 (1968–69): 94–126. *NT Abstracts* 16 (1968-69): 165. Holds for the historicity of the cry by the whole (assembled) people, in the spirit of a similar phrase in an anonymous Mishnah (*Sanh.* 4:5) still well known in the time of Christ.

Lietzmann, Hans. "Bemerkungen zum Prozess Jesu I." *ZNW* 30 (1931): 211-15.

Lohmeyer, Ernst. *Das Evangelium mach Markus,* 11th ed. Göttingen: Vandenhoeck & Ruprecht, 1951.

Lohse, Eduard. *History of the Suffering and Death of Jesus Christ.* Philadelphia: Fortress Press, 1967.

Mantel, Hugo. *Studies in the History of the Sanhedrin.* Cambridge: Harvard University Press, 1965.

Martinez, E. R. "The Gospel Accounts of the Death of Jesus: A Study of the Death Accounts Made in the Light of the New Testament Traditions, the Redaction and the Theology of the Four Evangelists." Dissertation, Pontifical Gregorian University, Rome, 1970.

Marxsen, Willi. *Mark the Evangelist: Studies in the Redaction History of the Gospel.* Nashville: Abingdon, 1951.

Moloney, Francis J., S.D.B. *The Gospel of John.* Collegeville, Minn.: Liturgical Press, 1998. See 481–515.

———. *The Gospel of Mark.* Peabody, MA: Hendrickson, 2002, 297–336.

O'Neill, J. C."The Charge of Blasphemy at Jesus' Trial before the Sanhedrin." In Bammel, ed., *Trial,* 72–77. The basis for the charge may have been Jesus' "temerity of using any title at all before God the Father had himself announced the enthronement of his anointed one."

———. "The Silence of Jesus." *NTS* 15 (1969–70): 153–67. *NT Abstracts* 13 (1969-70): 822.

Ramsey, A. Michael. *The Narratives of the Passion.* Contemporary Studies in Theology 1. London: Mowbray, 1962.

Rivkin, Ellis. *What Crucified Jesus? Messianism, Pharisaism, and the Development of Christianity.* Foreword by Eugene J. Fisher. New York: UAHC Press, 1997.

Ruckstuhl, Eugene. *Chronology of the Last Days of Jesus: A Critical Study.* New York: Desclée, 1965.

Sandmel, Samuel. "The Trial of Jesus: Reservations." *Judaism* 20 (1971): 69–74. Sandmel's views and their background are more fully spelled out in his book *A Jewish Understanding of the New Testament* (Cincinnati: Hebrew Union College, 1956, reprinted New York: Ktav, 1974).

Senior, Donald, C.P. *The Passion of Jesus in the Gospel of John.* Collegeville, Minn.: Liturgical Press, 1991.

———. *The Passion of Jesus in the Gospel of Luke.* Wilmington, Del.: Michael Glazier, 1989.

———. *The Passion of Jesus in the Gospel of Mark.* Wilmington, Del.: Michael Glazier, 1984.

———. *The Passion of Jesus in the Gospel of Matthew.* Wilmington, Del.: Michael Glazier, 1985.

Shepherd, Massey H., Jr. "Are Both the Synoptics and John Correct about the Date of Jesus' Death?" *JBL* 80 (1961): 123–32.

Sherwin-White, A. N. *Roman Society and Roman Law in The New Testament.* Sarum Lectures 1960–61. Oxford: Clarendon, 1963.

———. "The Trial of Christ." In *Historicity and Chronology in the New Testament.* Ed. D. E. Nineham et al. SPCK Theological Collections 6. London: SPCK, 1965, 97–116.

Sloyan, Gerard S. *The Crucifixion of Jesus: History, Myth, Faith.* Minneapolis: Fortress Press, 1995.

———. *Preaching from the Lectionary: An Exegetical Commentary with CD-Rom.* Minneapolis: Fortress Press, 2004.

———. *Why Jesus Died.* Minneapolis: Fortress Press, 2004; a partial abridgment of *The Crucifixion of Jesus.*

Swidler, Leonard, ed. "From Holocaust to Dialogue: A Jewish-Christian

Dialogue between Americans and Germans." *Journal of Ecumenical Studies* 18/1 (winter 1981): 1-142.

Taylor, Vincent. *The Gospel According to St. Mark.* London: Macmillan, 1955.

———. "The Narrative of the Crucifixion." *NTS* 8 (1961–62): 333–34.

———. "The Origin of the Markan Passion-Sayings." *NTS* 1 (1954–55): 159–67.

———. *The Passion Narrative of St. Luke: A Critical and Historical Investigation.* Ed. O. E. Evans. SNTSMS 19 (1972). See above p. 68 ff., and chap. 5, nn. 2-5.

Vawter, Bruce, C.M. "Are the Gospels Anti-Semitic?" *Journal of Ecumenical Studies* 5 (1968): 473–87. *NT Abstracts* 13 (1968): 530.

Wilson, R. McL. "The New *Passion of Jesus* in the Light of the New Testament and Apocrypha." In *Neotestamentica et Semitica: Studies in Honour of Matthew Black.* Eds. E. Earle Ellis and Max Wilcox. Edinburgh: T. & T. Clark, 1969, 264–71. Wilson discusses on the text of the *Passion of Jesus* published in Shlomo Pines, "The Jewish Christians of the Early Centuries of Christianity according to a New Source," *Proceedings of the Israel Academy of Sciences and Humanities* 2, 13 (Jerusalem, 1966). See also Robert Kraft, *JBL* 86 (1967): 329, and A. T. Nikolainen, *NTS* 14 (1967–68): 287–89. The Arabic text, from the Muslim 'Abd al-Jabbār (tenth century CE), gives two passion accounts, one similar to John, the other seemingly intensifying Jewish responsibility (the Jews seize Jesus from the prison where Herod placed him overnight and torture and crucify him).

Wilson, William R. *The Execution of Jesus: A Judicial, Literary and Historical Investigation.* New York: Scribner's, 1970.

Winter, Paul. "The Markan Account of Jesus' Trial by the Sanhedrin," *JTS* NS14 (1963): 94–102.

———. *On the Trial of Jesus.* Berlin: de Gruyter, 1961. Winter argues against the likelihood of any Jewish trial—John 18:19-24, the hearing before Annas, comes from the fourth Evangelist; Mark 14:53b, 55-64, the Sanhedrin trial, is "editorial accretion due to the Second Evangelist"; Luke 22:67-71, details about a morning session by the Sanhedrin to examine (not try) Jesus (and which does not pass any death sentence), seems imported from Matthew, with possible post-Lukan adaptions; only Mark 15:1 = Luke 22:66, 23:1, a deliberation in the Sanhedrin's Council Hall, in the early morning, resulting in his being sent to Pilate, can be called primary tradition.

———. "The Treatment of His Sources by the Third Evangelist in Luke xxi to xxiv," *Studia Theologica* 8 (1955): 138–72.

———. "Zum Prozess Jesu" in Eckert, *Antijudaismus im NTZ* (1967), 95–104.

GENERAL INDEX

Abraham, 81, 96

Annas, 13, 57, 86, 88, 90, 93, 95, 101

Anointing of Jesus at Bethany, 85, 88

Antiochus IV Epiphanes, 39

Apocalyptic writing, 59

Apologetic purpose of Christians, 2, 7, 22, 24, 82, 100, 103

Arrest (Gethsemane), 24, 33, 52, 53, 70, 88, 92f

Augustus, 20, 27

Authority (*imperium*) of a prefect, 20

Bacon, B.W., 65

Bar Kokhba, 7, 46

Barabbas, 25, 50f, 63, 64, 73, 75, 86, 90, 101

Blasphemy, 5, 35, 46

Blood of Jesus invoked as claim of innocence, 66

"Books of testimonies," 39

Brandon, S.G.F., 6f, 23, 31, 140

Brown, Raymond E., 113, 140

Bultmann, Rudolf, 24f, 33, 34, 47f, 49, 140

Caiaphas, 13, 57, 88, 90, 93, 95, 101

Caligula, 21

Catchpole, D.R., 48, 113, 128, 130, 135

Chief priests, 34, 35, 51, 53, 58, 62, 66, 71, 76, 82, 87, 90, 100, 131
  See also Priesthood, opposition to Jesus of

"Christ, the Son of the Blessed," 5, 37, 44

Civil (political) charges against Jesus, 17, 72, 75, 77f, 81f

Claudius, 18, 20

Coponius, 17, 20

Defilement, ritual, 26

Divine/heavenly man (*theîos anēr*), 32, 52, 55, 89

Egypt, governors (prefects) of, 20, 50

Elders, 26, 53, 62, 70, 76, 101, 102

Elijah/Elisha, Jesus as, 89

Enoch, 39, 41

Eschatological concern, 41f, 42f, 68f

Exaltation (enthronement) of Christ, 37f, 42-44, 78f, 80

Field of Blood, 62

Florus, Gessius, 27

"Formula quotations," 62

"Friend of Caesar"
  See Philokaisar

145

INDEX OF SCRIPTURE PASSAGES

CPSIA information can be obtained at www.ICGtesting.com
Printed in the USA
269355BV00009B/1/P